Other Books by Victor C. Bolles

Principled Policy, A Conversation about America

Edifice of Trust, Second Edition

Tawantinsuyu, A novel about nuclear terror

A Summation of the Principles of Taxation

2017
A Trumpian Year in Review

by Victor C. Bolles

Copyright © by Victor C. Bolles

All rights reserved. No part of this book may be reproduced in any form or by any electronic or mechanical means, including information storage and retrieval systems, without permission in writing from the publisher except by a reviewer who may quote brief passages in a review.

Table of Contents

January 2017   1
    Greed is
    The Never Ending Election
    Flip or Flop
    What's More Important Than Safety

February 2017   19
    Warning Signs
    Principles of Taxation I
    Principles of Taxation II
    Principles of Taxation III

March 2017   50
    unbrandedcare
    I Dream of Gini

April 2017   63
    The Opioid Economy
    The Weight of the World
    Our Jackie
    Vive le Difference
    A Principled Analysis of the Trump Tax Reform Plan

May 2017   94
    Windage
    With Great Fanfare

June 2017   101
    I Don't Want Your Damn Help, Al
    Heartless
    A Bold Idea (about Taxes)

July 2017 — 118
    Not Too Much to Ask For
    In Praise of Self-Interest
    Righteous Thinking and Foolish Nature
    ZombieCare

August 2017 — 140
    RAISE-ing a Ruckus
    Bias vs. Bias
    Robt E. Lee
    What is Winning

September 2017 — 160
    BernieCare is Your Right
    Reaganesque? Not Quite
    This is Dumb!

October 2017 — 175
    The Nudger Laureate
    Catatonica

November 2017 — 186
    Making Diversity Work
    The Elephant in the Room
    Progressivism Confronts Human Nature

December 2017 — 200
    Wagner's Sad Law
    Grading the GOP Tax Bill

Putting a Tumultuous Year in Perspective — 213

2017: A Trumpian Year in Review

January 2017

Greed is........

January 4, 2017
Victor C. Bolles

Greed is.....

We all know how to complete this phrase. Mimicking Gordon Gekko (who was in turn mimicking – or actually paraphrasing - Ivan Boesky) from the 1980's film *Wall Street*, "Greed is good." But greed is a sin, one of the Seven Deadly sins. And as we all know from Sister Mary Margaret's well-wielded ruler, sin is bad.

Greed, like all the Seven Deadly Sins (and many others which are presumably less lethal), has been around for a very long time. From the book of Proverbs, King Solomon is supposed to have written that "six things doth the LORD hate: yea, seven are an abomination unto him." I would venture to guess that the concept of sin has been with us equally as long as the concept of good behavior.

2017: A Trumpian Year in Review

Many leftists (Progressives, socialists and far-left Democrats) assert that greed is the essence of the capitalist economic system. They believe that Gordon Gekko's phrase is what all Wall Streeters feel in their heart of hearts and how they conduct their business. They believe that greed and contempt for the concerns of other people drives the entire capitalist machine.

I don't think that is the case but that's not the point. Greed and the other sins, deadly or not, are part of our human make-up and have been with us since time immemorial – long before "capitalism." It is part of our human nature: strong in some, less in others, but always there. It doesn't matter what economic system we live under, greed will be present.

The beauty of the free market economic system (a description I think more accurately describes our current economic system than "capitalism") is that the motives of the economic players are irrelevant to the benefits that society receives from economic activity. To repeat Adam Smith once again, "It is not from the benevolence of the butcher, the brewer, or the baker that we expect our dinner, but from their regard to their own interest." It doesn't matter if the butcher, brewer or baker is greedy or not. What is in his (or her) heart is irrelevant as long as the product is healthy, functions as claimed, is not defective and at a reasonable price as a result of competition from other butchers, brewers and bakers.

In our democratic social contract actions that harm or infringe on the rights of others are subject to legal recourse. Malevolent thoughts that are not acted upon are not punishable. So even though a merchant or businessman might be motivated by greed, if that person acts within the rules and regulations established by society there is no actionable cause. If fear of sanction by society prevents a person from acting on sinful thoughts; he (or she) might have problems when meeting his (or her) maker, but will not have problem before a judge.

Leftists of all stripes will deny that motives don't matter. Motives are all that matter to leftists. They believe they are good people and that they do what they do because they want to do good. I also believe that they are (mostly) good people and that they want to do good. But their focus on motives makes them misidentify the cause of the inequities they perceive in the streets of America and around the world. And if you misidentify the cause of a problem, your proposed solution will not work.

Greed will still be present in the government-dominated societies that our progressive friends offer as solutions to the injustice in the world. But greedy people will not be found on Wall Street or in large privately owned corporations because such entities will cease to exist as the government dominates all economic activities. Greedy people will gravitate to government and state-owned enterprises (SOEs) because that is where their greed can be satiated. The problem in these government dominated societies is that there is no other institution to counter-balance government or expose the corrupt actions of these greedy individuals. Rather than expose and solve problems, government covers them up (just look at what is happening in Malaysia as well as Brazil and Venezuela right now).

Countries where government is supreme are notoriously corrupt. Apparatchiks live like princes, managers of SOEs loot their companies. Shoddy and defective products flood the market at prices set by a committee of bureaucrats. Consumers that seek a solution to this dilemma are labeled economic saboteurs and criminals.

The problem we face in America is not that there are greedy people that are violating our rules and regulations; it is that these people have, in collusion with government, structured the rules and regulations such that these greedy actions are within the bounds of the law. Because the American social contract has been warped to the benefit of favored elites that can influence government, the people have lost trust in the system. The unique thing about America is that the people once had faith and trust in the American government. Most of the people on this planet have never had any trust in their government and are completely resigned to their fate. We still believe we can change things.

It is the rules of society that define how people are to act. The government is charged with creating a framework of laws and regulations that manage how the social contract functions. But the goal of this framework of laws and regulations should not be to punish the greedy bastards for their sins. Instead, the goal of the social contract (and its framework of rules and regulations) is to build the trust of citizens in their interactions, economic and social, with other citizens. So the goal of regulation is not to punish evil-doers (although sanctions do play a role in the Rule of Law) or put business in a straightjacket but to restore trust in economic interactions and promote economic growth.

2017: A Trumpian Year in Review

President Elect Trump promises to get rid of many of the onerous rules and regulations decreed by the Obama administration that are strangling the economic recovery. These regulations impose an especially deleterious effect on small businesses because of the high costs of compliance. But to give a free hand to base motives will not build trust in the economic system. Reducing the approximately 10,000 employees of the Food Safety and Inspection Service to 5,000 would save the government a lot of money and give a freer hand to meat and food producers but wouldn't necessarily increase the public's trust in the products of these companies and would, thus, be counterproductive (especially as people start to keel over from salmonella poisoning). Smart regulation designed to foster trust in our economic system would promote economic growth and create jobs. If Mr. Trump attempts to restore trust through direct personal action (as he has often done via Twitter) he will create an edifice of sand that will wash away once he sheds this mortal coil (or leaves office). If he wants to build a legacy for the history books he will reform and rebuild the American democratic institutions and restore the America Social Contract.

<u>2018 Perspective</u>: President Trump's reduction and elimination of rules and regulations has had a very positive economic impact without any negative side effects as of yet. Only time will tell. It has been good to roll back the excessive anti-business regulation of the Obama era but regulation still has a role to play in maintaining the social contract.

The Never Ending Election

January 20, 2017
Victor C. Bolles

As of now, some sixty odd Democrats have stated publicly their intention to boycott the inauguration of Donald Trump on Friday, January 20th. I don't want to go into the media battle between Mr. Trump and Representative John Lewis that has flowed from Rep. Lewis' interview on one of the Sunday talking-heads shows where he stated that he felt that Mr. Trump's election was not legitimate (he apparently felt the same about the election of George W. Bush as well).

Democrats are trying to come up with a reason their candidate, Hillary Clinton, lost other than the fact that she and her team ran a terrible campaign and lost the votes of a vast swath of people across the country (especially the center of the country). They cite Russian hacking, FBI investigations, white supremacy, the Electoral College and the kitchen sink. These dedicated Clintonites feel worse than Dallas fans after last Sunday's game. How could their candidate have lost? She had everything: minorities, women (considered a minority although they make up 50.8% of the population), abortion, gun violence, experience, everything. It goes on and on. How could she lose?

They think there has to be a reason for this unbelievable outcome. They had a lock. They had the Democratic National Committee packing things in their favor. They had the media feeding her debate questions. They had pay-for-play. Their opponent was a pussy-grabbing buffoon who tweets before he thinks. What could go wrong?

The psychological straw they are grabbing at is to deny that the election is over and that Mr. Trump will be a legitimate President. Clinton Campaign Chairman Leon Podesta refused to concede Trump's victory during interviews after the election. Leftist operative David Brock declared "Our goal is to keep Trump unpopular" according to Buzzfeed (as if he needed help).

What I would like to know is what possible good do these Democrats think will result from delegitimizing the Trump presidency? It might make them feel better to continually bash Mr. Trump. He is likely to be a cornucopia of opportunities for criticism. Bashing Trump and trying to frustrate any and all of his policies might make them feel superior to the supposed idiots that elected him. Go ahead. It's the American way.

But would delegitimizing the election serve the American people? Attacking Mr. Trump's election isn't attacking Mr. Trump. It is attacking the US and our democratic institutions. Attacking the 45th peaceful transition of power unnerves the American people and gives comfort to our enemies. Unfortunately for the Dems, the Electoral College functioned exactly as the Founders intended.

Oh, and by the way, their frantic efforts to delegitimize Mr. Trump's election are blown away by the fact that they also lost the House, the Senate, the governorships and most state legislatures.

2018 Perspective. Nothing has changed. Democrats still are trying to delegitimize the Trump presidency although their focus now is impeachment. Even though they lost most of the center of the country, the Democrats are moving even further left in the run up to the 2018 elections.

Flip or Flop

January 26, 2017
Victor C. Bolles

Prior to the election I predicted that there would be a plethora of opportunities to write about for the next four years no matter who got elected and, boy, was I right! Just this week I can choose from alternative facts, Trans-Pacific Partnership (TPP), massive voter fraud investigations, border taxes, it goes on and on.

One cause of all this controversy is Mr. Trump's notoriously thin skin combined with his enormous ego. This toxic combination makes him burst into paroxysms of twitter posts at the least slight of his power or popularity. He is obsessed with poll ratings, attendance numbers and twitter followers (he's way behind former President Obama). He even made a point to note that Arnold Schwarzenegger's ratings on the Celebrity Apprentice weren't as good as his. Everything is a contest and he always has to win.

But the question we must ask ourselves is if Mr. Trump's outrageous vanity will impair his ability to lead the country? History tells us that many other great leaders had serious character flaws while many decent, honest, well-intentioned leaders failed miserably. Mr. Trump's thin skin reminds me of Alexander Hamilton whose fatally thin skin led him to duel it out with Aaron Burr. Despite his character flaws Hamilton was a brilliant leader who established the Treasury Department and our US financial system at the founding of our country.

Alexander Hamilton was the right man at the right time. Seriously flawed Winston Churchill rose to the occasion as Britain's wartime leader. The United States is itself in a time of transition from being the world leader that won both the Second World War and the Cold War to what? We all feel that we are in a time of transition but we don't know exactly where we are going or how to get there. But we do know that the path that we were on was unsustainable and that a new paradigm was needed.

One of my favorite shows on TV is Flip or Flop. It's about two young real estate agents who purchase run-down houses, fix them up and then sell them for a profit. But this is way different than speculators who buy houses and then resell them at higher prices without adding any value. When Tarek and Christina go into a run-down house they tear down and rip out all the rotten wood and linoleum, bring electrical and plumbing up to code and convert old stodgy room arrangements into wide-open modern homes. It can cost them up to $100,000 to renovate some of these houses but with their efforts and design ideas they usually make a profit.

2017: A Trumpian Year in Review

Any major transition requires the demolition of the old in order to build the new. In his first few days in office, Mr. Trump has shown he has the ability to tear things down. He has undone many of President Obama's executive orders and promises to do more. He has rattled our allies and threatened our trade partners. He has intimidated as well as cajoled domestic manufacturers. No one knows what's coming next but they are all getting prepared for a new world order.

It will likely be impossible to stop President Trump from tearing down much of the current order. But it would be unwise and counterproductive to block him from putting something new in place of the old. He is a good negotiator and this may be one of his negotiating tactics. We need to see some of the new policies and how they work before we are in a position to judge. Let's see if he can build us a shiny new edifice out of a crumbling shack. If he builds a load of crap or nothing at all leaving chaos in his wake, at least we can change things in four years.

2018 Perspective: President Trump is still in the demolition phase of the renovation. We still have no clear picture on what the renovation will look like. Hopefully at the end of four years we will have something other than wreckage.

What's More Important Than Safety?

January 30, 2017
Victor C. Bolles

President Donald Trump's executive actions to insure the safety of Americans (plus his off the cuff commentary) have stirred up worldwide controversy. First, there was the wall and who would pay for it. Next was the ban on US entry from some (but not all) Muslim countries. And there were also televised comments about his acceptance of the use of torture and waterboarding (although he deferred to his

Secretary of Defense Gen. Mattis on this matter who is opposed). President Trump said our enemies use these techniques and that we have to be smart and tough in order to keep Americans safe. You will note that he did not say that we have to be principled or that we have to honor American traditions and Western values. He must think that these attributes are only for losers. And he hates losing.

His rationale for spending around $10 billion to erect a wall between the United States and Mexico (and have Mexico pay for it) is based on the assumption that this will keep out illegal immigrants and especially criminals. But the land border between the US and Mexico is 1,989 miles while total US border and coastlines are 19,894 miles. The Mexican border represents only 10% of the potential for illegal entry (17% if you eliminate the 8,178 miles of Alaskan borders and coastline). While it is true that criminals cross the southern border to commit crimes and import drugs because it is easy, it would be naïve to think that a wall would deter them when there are so many other opportunities available (and the wall wouldn't stop the tunnels they like to dig). Add in the fact that about 30 to 40 percent of illegal immigrants entered the US legally and have overstayed their visas and you will realize that the wall is at best only a partial solution. There are much better, smarter ways to solve this problem in a way to improve US security. Electronic tracking of visas and Social Security linked ID cards would make it difficult for illegals to hide out or get employment. Nothing is absolute but there are a lot of things we can do to mitigate the problem without building a wall. A wall is a simplistic approach to a complex problem (and it will destroy the views from Big Bend National Park).

The rhetoric about forcing Mexico to pay for the wall is already backfiring. The method for extracting payment from the Mexicans has not yet been determined so it is moot to go into a detailed discussion of the possible repercussions but it is safe to say that Americans will also suffer from the eventual policy. But is treating Mexicans like dirt likely to enhance our security? It is stupid to think that Mexicans will say, "Somos mexicanos. Nos encanta ser tratados como la suciedad (We're Mexicans. We love being treated like dirt.)." People deserve dignity. Don't you think our security would be enhanced by having a friendly, prosperous neighbor on our southern border than an angry neighbor forced into alignment with our other international antagonists? Then we might really need a wall. We could call it "Maginot".

While it is reasonable to increase scrutiny of people coming to our country from war zones and state sponsors of terror, does an outright ban on all citizens from seven countries (Iraq, Iran, Syria, Somalia, Libya, Sudan and Yemen) increase our safety and security? The US is an international center for business, finance and diplomacy and many of the people coming to our shores are businessmen and diplomats with valid visas (many international institutions such as the UN, the IMF and the World Bank have employees from all over the world working in the US but if you want to kick out all those institutions, what the heck!). Many other travelers have relatives that are citizens and legal residents. I guess if all these people look like nails then all you need is a hammer. But banning citizens from these and potentially other countries undermines our ability to be an international anything. I can understand the urge to consider America First but I would be afraid of America Alone.

President Trump has publicly endorsed the use of waterboarding and other unnamed torture techniques in order to make America safer provoking domestic and international outrage. Secretary of Defense Mattis rejects those techniques and states that skillful interrogation can obtain better intelligence than the use of torture. I would agree, given sufficient time. But when time is of the essence, does waterboarding or torture save lives? No better authority than Khalid Sheikh Mohammed says that any jihadi who provides useful intelligence without being forced by torture is condemned to eternal hell. And former head of the CIA Michael Hayden says that they had obtained useful intelligence from waterboarding of KSM and two others. But does the use of torture make America safer? While the use of torture might prevent certain specific acts of terror and save American lives, its use will undermine America's standing in the world as the leader of the West and the champion of Western values and ideals. It was these values and ideals that included the ban on torture in the Geneva Conventions. The Bush administration's legal dance to differentiate between torture and enhanced interrogation notwithstanding, the use of torture is prohibited by our Western ideals and values no matter how efficacious it might be. The breakdown of the international order established by the US in the wake of World War II would jeopardize many more American lives than could be saved by the use of torture.

These proposals to insure the safety of Americans are an example of President Trump following through on his campaign promises (something which politicians rarely do). But many of those campaign promises were made off the cuff in the heat primary battles as then-candidate Trump spoke at his famously unscripted rallies. Following through on campaign promises might be considered an honorable thing to do but one would hope that now-President Trump would take the opportunity to study and understand the more complex realities of these situations and the possible consequences of these actions.

President Trump does not view things on a principled basis but on a transactional one. In business you bargain hard to get a deal done but if it doesn't work out you pass on it and move on to the next deal. As the Swiss say, money has no smell. It's just business (bidness here in Texas). No harm no foul.

But that's not how it works in international relations. The Mexican people and their government are going to remember this wall incident for a long time no matter how it is resolved (as Mary Anastasia O'Grady noted in her column they still chafe at the Treaty of Guadalupe Hidalgo and that was 169 years ago). And people from the Middle East and the Muslim world are not going to think that travel bans and enhanced interrogation are examples of America being tough and smart but that our professed Western values are nothing but a sham that we shed when convenient.

Our Western values have evolved in fits and starts over a period of two thousand years. There have been periods of cruelty and horror such as the Crusades, the

Inquisition, slavery, colonialism and genocide of indigenous peoples. But over time we have matured as a culture although we are still imperfect. After the convulsions of two world wars we have had a period of relative peace for 70 years because Western values under American leadership have governed international relations. This may seem counter-intuitive to some of you but remember that all the casualties of the wars in Afghanistan and Iraq pale in comparison the losses of those world wars. Not all the world agreed with our Western values but most nations have been (relatively) content to live under those concepts because they have worked. The world is now a more peaceful and prosperous place than ever before. But this peace has become more fragile as America under President Obama stepped back from its leadership role. President Trump, citing its costs, is urging a further reduction of our leadership role. More than that he is urging us to turn our backs on our Western values and adopt the methods and strategies of those that hate America and its values. By ignoring the principles on which America was founded, President Trump is doing the work of those that oppose us.

2018 Perspective. President Trump continues to tear down all the international institutions created at the end of World War Two to institute an American world order. However, he does not appear to have a new order to replace the old, worn-out Bretton Woods institutions. I don't feel safer. Do you?

February 2017

Warning Signs

February 9, 2017
Victor C. Bolles

Donald J. Trump @realDonaldTrump Feb 5

Just cannot believe a judge would put our country in such peril. If something happens blame him and court system. People pouring in. Bad!

How does a country slide from freedom into authoritarianism? What are the telltale signs? History gives us numerous examples.

The rise of Hitler to power is instructive. Hitler in 1930 had previously attempted a violent overthrow of the Weimar government (the "Putsch") and served time in jail during which he wrote Mein Kampf (My Struggle). Extreme factions on the right and left beset the German parliament (Reichstag) in 1930 and the minority centrist government was unable to deal with the impact of the Great Depression or other problems. Hitler ran against Hindenburg for the office of President and he lost although, with the help of his hard-core supporters, he came in second with a vote of over 35%. With a government unable to address pressing problems, prominent Germans urged Hindenburg to appoint Hitler as chancellor, which he did. Hitler was able to maneuver the Reichstag to pass a law to grant him the ability to rule by decree. He quickly took over the labor unions and other democratic institutions and, when Hindenburg died in 1934, took full power as Fuhrer (leader). Elections continued to be held but with only Nazi candidates.

The rise of Hugo Chavez was eerily similar. Like Hitler, Chavez led an abortive attempt to overthrow the democratic government of Venezuela in 1992. In an attempt to calm rising tensions in the country, a weak centrist government liberated him after only a few years in prison. Chavez immediately set out campaigning for the next presidential election, which he was able to win handily. Riding a wave of popularity he rewrote the Venezuelan Constitution that increased the number of Supreme Court justices, allowed the president to rule by decree, extended the presidential term and allowed reelection, and granted additional executive powers while eviscerating the legislature. He used state media to promote his personality cult, started his own newspapers and TV channel and drove independent media out of business. He continued to have elections but the Chavez government tightened its grip on the media and arrested opposition candidates. Only death could end his grip on power.

From these two examples of populist authoritarianism (one from the left and one from the right) we can begin to discern patterns (although I am sure there are many other examples out there).

In order to get into power:

1. Take advantage of a weak and/or ineffective centrist government

2. Increase the radicalization of the right and left wings

3. Use, but do not believe in, democracy

4. Election by massive voting by a block of supporters

5. Intimidation of opponents (by Brown Shirts in Germany and by colectivos in Venezuela)

Once in power in order to assure continuance in power:

1. Rule by decree

2. Change constitution or pass enabling legislation

3. Control and/or politicize Supreme Court

4. Communicate directly with the people though state media

5. Undermine and eliminate independent media

6. Take over independent trade unions

7. continue sham elections

8. Demonize minorities

9. Ramp up fear of attack in order to justify emergency war powers

In the twenty-first century we have seen similar kinds of patterns beginning to take shape in the United States. Both the Republican and Democratic Parties are held in thrall by their far-out extremist elements. Compromise is now considered treason and worthy of expulsion from the party. The net result has been a weak and indecisive government that can't even pass a budget bill let alone major reform legislation. The 2016 elections were acrimonious and fraught with accusations of manipulation and abuse. We are inundated with fake news and alternative facts.

Only a few weeks in office, President Trump has been impugning the courts and the media of malfeasance and dishonesty. He has been lashing out on Twitter against those opposed to his policies while alienating long-time US allies with threats of altering or backing out of long-standing treaties. How different is America First from Deutschland uber alles?

In the above Tweet, President Trump is basically saying that the courts will be responsible for the next terror attack because they oppose his ban on immigration from seven state sponsors of terror. While it looks likely that he will prevail eventually (the law is pretty clear) he is undermining and weakening one of the three branches of government. The Founders created these three branches of government as a check on state power. Weakening, politicizing and controlling the courts are among the first actions that emerging dictators undertake. Of course, it was Franklin Roosevelt that first tried packing the court in order to assure that his New Deal legislation wouldn't be found unconstitutional (but he was blocked by Congress).

President Trump hasn't made any overt moves in this direction but we must remain on alert. His tweets show the disdain in which he holds his opponents. We do not know what course he might attempt to make if one of his major policy initiatives is held up or blocked by the courts or the legislature. Combining his attacks on the court system along with his vicious attacks on so-called mainstream media (now called just MSM) we see unnerving similarities to the strategies of authoritarian populists of both the left and the right.

Right now it seems he is just venting his spleen. His treatment of district judges is equivalent to the tongue lashing Nordstrom received from dropping his daughter's clothing line. We do not know if these are the ravings of a vain insecure person or the devious machinations of a person with a lust for power. But they are warnings signs. We must not gloss over these tendencies or our freedom will be in peril.

2018 Perspective. President Trump seems to hold all institutions in disdain but he has made some good (although conservative) selections to the Supreme Court. He also seems less prone to rule by decree (called executive order in the United States) than his predecessor, President Obama). Hitler and Chavez moved quickly to consolidate their power. If President Trump has any grand elaborate plans to overthrow American democracy he has made no overt moves so far (and based on his other policy initiatives he does not seem to be into grand elaborate plans as a rule).

Principles of Taxation I

February 14, 2017
Victor C. Bolles

It is not yet possible to critique President Trump's tax reform package that he is expected to announce in the next 2-3 weeks. Analysis of this reform package (which President Trump has said will be phenomenal) will be an interesting exercise. President Trump's Office of Management and Budget (OMB) says that the 2017 deficit will be $443 billion, a reduction of around 20% compared to the 2016 deficit of $552 billion. This will be accomplished by a 7.3% increase in tax revenues while expenditures increase only 3.1%. Of course, the 2017 budget is pretty much already cooked as we are already in the fifth month of the fiscal year. Looking forward to 2018 is inherently more speculative but OMB projects a further deficit reduction on a 5% increase in revenue against only a 3% increase in expenditures. But this is all before President Trump's phenomenal tax cut. It is also before promised increases in military spending, infrastructure projects and the continuation untouched of the major transfer programs such as Social Security and Medicare.

During the campaign, Mr. Trump stated that he was going to bring down the deficit "big league and quickly". When queried on how he stated that he would cut the budgets of the Department of Education and EPA. But these agencies only represent 2% of the total budget so it is hard to imagine how he would be able to bring down the deficit big league and quickly. The only people to play more fast and loose with financial projections than real estate developers are politicians so we are delving into some real big league hogwash here.

But in anticipation of some real gravity defying leaps of logic in the upcoming phenomenal tax reform proposal, let's think a bit about what we really want in a tax package.

First of all, let me state unequivocally my opposition of much of the received wisdom regarding taxes. To Republicans, the best way to spur economic growth is to cut taxes and then blindly trust that the Laffer curve will take care of resulting deficits. To Democrats, taxes are best utilized, not to fund government operations, but to extract undeserved wealth from the rich to give to deserving

Democratic-leaning voting blocs. They are both wrong. The key principles to ethically utilize the government's ability to tax its citizens are:

1. Taxes should be used to pay for the operations of government.

2. Incomprehensible tax rules undermine the people's trust in government so tax policy should be made understandable to citizens

3. It is not possible to create a tax system that will deemed to be "fair".

4. Payment of taxes is an obligation of citizenship so all citizens should pay some tax.

5. Tax policy should not be used to manipulate people or organizations.

6. Cutting taxes is not an effective means of generating long-term economic growth.

7. Corporate taxes should be competitive with the tax systems of our major trade partners.

8. Economic growth is stunted by uncertainty so tax policy should not change every year.

Adequate analysis of these principles will far exceed the optimum length for a blog post of this type. And discussion of these principles also leads to many additional important issues that need to be discussed as well. So we will attack this subject in a piecemeal, but orderly and logical, fashion. For a more in-depth discussion of this topic, I suggest you pick up a copy of my book, *Principled Policy*, which is available on Amazon and other outlets.

The Purpose of Taxation

So let us take up first, the purpose of taxation. The Founders of our country, after existing a few years under the Articles of Confederation, soon learned that a government that lacks the ability to tax will quickly perish. According to the theory of the social contract as developed by Enlightenment philosophers, citizens cede a portion of their natural rights to government so that the government has the ability maintain the functionality of the social contract. Government needs coercive power to force the payment of taxes in order to guarantee its continued existence and, thereby, the continuation of the social contract that citizens have agreed to.

The cession of certain natural rights by citizens empowers the federal government to enforce laws and collect taxes. In the preamble to the Constitution, the government is also obligated to provide services to the citizens in exchange for this cession of natural rights. In summation, the entirety of all these obligations of the government is to maintain the functionality of the social contract according to its founding principles (unless those principles are changed by the will of the people). The purpose of the taxes citizens pay is to provide the government the ability to fulfill these obligations.

The current lack of trust in government is prima facie evidence that the government has not lived up to its obligations to properly maintain the functionality of the social contract. Trust is the most essential element of the social contract. It is the lack of trust in our interactions with other human beings that motivates us to form social organizations bound by a social contract. Lacking trust, the whole fabric of society begins to unravel.

Toward a Comprehensible Tax System

The current tax code is so complex that there are very few people who understand it in its entirety. This fact alone is a breach of the obligations imposed on the government by the social contract. Much of this complexity arises from sections of the tax code that benefit private interests. Other complexities arise from special benefits or subsidies intended to promote certain government-approved activities such as a tax credit to purchase a plug-in electric car or install solar panels.

But all these benefits, subsidies and deductions clutter up the tax code. In addition to making the tax code complex, using the tax code to provide such benefits muddies up government accounting. Do we actually know how much the plug-in electric car benefit for Tesla cars costs the American public? A hard-working investigator with knowledge of the tax code and oodles of time could probably figure this out (or at least give a good estimate). But for most of us, we haven't a clue.

The thing is, all of these tax benefits could be done in a different way. Instead of giving a tax credit just give purchasers of plug-in electric vehicles the cash instead. Of course this would require Congress to approve an appropriation for this expenditure and the expense would go directly to the expenditures report when calculating the annual deficit instead of lurking safely behind the fog of taxes not collected (the Congressional Budget Office estimates these so-called tax expenditures cost the federal government $1.5 trillion in 2015). But such a simple solution would result in greater accounting transparency of the government, which our public servants try to avoid. Using the tax code also allows the benefit to keep on giving without annual appropriations which might prompt somebody to say, why the hell are we still wasting money on that?"

There is another thing that confuses me and maybe you as well. The Constitution obligates the government to do certain things to maintain the functionality of the social contract. These functions are essential as it builds the trust of citizens in their economic transactions with other citizens and promotes economic growth. Fulfilling these functions costs money and that is why government is empowered to collect taxes.

But in governmentese these constitutionally mandated functions are described as "discretionary expenditures" while transfers of wealth between citizens that are not contemplated in the Constitution are deemed "mandatory expenditures". In fact, such mandatory expenditures have grown to be more than half of the federal budget and are crowding out discretionary expenditures that are constitutionally mandated.

The government does have an obligation to payout much of these "mandatory expenditures" because people have been paying into these programs all their lives. I have been paying into Social Security for over 50 years and into Medicare since its inception. I had no choice in the matter; the government forced me to make those payments (except for when I worked for the C&O/B&O when I paid into the Railroad Retirement Fund). It would be an injustice to deny benefits to retirees who have been paying into Social Security and Medicare for decades.

So our problem is not that these social welfare payments exist (that discussion would be lengthy and not directly relevant to our discussion of taxes) but how to develop a tax system to address these enormous and mounting obligations. Because money is fungible, government has been using the money paid into these programs for other government expenditures instead of setting them aside in order to fund their ability to provide future benefits. This worked well for the government for many years as payments received exceeded disbursements for benefits. This fortuitous relationship has changed and the government is now depleting the accumulated notional trust funds and will soon be forced to use general tax revenue to fund these benefits. This mixing of operating expenditures and social welfare transfers is confusing (I think purposefully so). I think that dedicating our social welfare contribution to those functions and not mixing them with operating expenses would greatly clarify the tax system. Of course, not allowing government to easily move money around the system would have an impact on how to fund these programs on a sustainable basis.

Trust in government is near all time lows. There are many reasons for this lack of trust and tax reform will not solve this problem. But taxation is one of the raw nerve endings that really gets people worked up. Trust in government is an essential element of the social contract without which the social contract begins to break down. Increasing the public's trust in the tax system would be a positive first step in restoring the American Social Contract.

In the next essay on taxation we will start by addressing the issue of "fairness." What fun!

2018 Perspective. See my essay, Grading the GOP Tax Bill, December 22, 2017.

Principles of Taxation II

February 15, 2017
Victor C. Bolles

In our first discussion on the principles of taxation I elaborated on the importance of the government's ability to tax its citizens in order to finance the functions necessary to support the social contract. I also argued that greater clarity and transparency in the tax system would increase the public's trust in the tax system that has been undermined by the current complexity and opaqueness of the tax code. In this second essay on the principles of taxation I want to discuss why I think it is impossible to create a "fair" tax system.

On Fairness

Dr. Daniel Kahneman in his book *Thinking Fast and Slow* (based on his research along with his long time partner Amos Tversky) asserts that the human brain consists of two systems but I could never keep them straight. I call System One (which is quick thinking and intuitive) our instinctual brain while I call System Two our rational and scientific brain that is controlled by reason (and justifies our species being called homo sapiens or wise man). The instinctual brain is more related to the survival instincts of our hominid and great ape ancestors. Kahneman further asserts that while the rational brain is what makes us human it is also lazy and is only called to action when necessary. The rest of time the instinctual brain is in charge.

The instinctual brain is the fast part of thinking fast and slow. For primitive man, hesitation on the savannah or the tundra could be the difference between life and death. If it were not for our instinctual brain we would not have survived as a species long enough to become rational. But many of our biases and prejudices lie in the instinctual brain because they were necessary for survival in the primitive world but are an impediment in our current more civilized world.

I believe that the concept of fairness lies deep within the instinctual brain. A pack animal that does not get its fair share of the hunt does not survive. This relation to survival also explains the visceral reaction to perceived unfairness. We have all seen the pack or pride consuming the fresh meat from the hunt, snarling and snapping at others in the pack (and any other interlopers like vultures or hyenas) to make sure they get their "fair' share.

Humans do not initially learn about fairness in the pew or classroom. We learn it on the playground long before we become self-aware. Not a lot of snarling or snapping but a lot of crying and running to mommy to complain about perceived unfairness.

I have been told that the sense of fairness is part of our innate goodness as human beings and that it underlies many of our religious principles and perceptions of civilized behavior. That may be, but that does not alter its savage origins.

Whether it is innate or instinctual, fairness is subjective. There is no such thing as universal fairness. Fairness is personal. A sense of fairness can be shared by many people if it matches their specific circumstances or shared belief systems. But when their circumstances change or when there is a different belief system this shared sense of fairness can evaporate. A ref's call can be fair or unfair depending on if you are a Packers' or a Cowboys' fan no matter if you share the same religious or educational background.

Tax Fairness

Drs. Kahneman and Tversky had many insightful revelations about how humans react to various situations that they elaborated into the Prospect Theory for which Kahneman won the Nobel Prize in Economics (having passed away Tversky did not receive a prize because these prizes are not awarded posthumously – hey! That's not fair!). A critical aspect of Prospect Theory is the concept of loss aversion. Kahneman and Tversky asserted that people feel losses more than gains. Gains are pleasing but losses hurt – a lot.

Taxation is a taking of one's personal property through the use of coercive force by government. It is inherently unfair from the perspective of the taxpayer. It takes a force of will to summon the rational brain to realize that this payment is for the greater good of society and that, as an individual, you benefit from a smooth running society. It is even a benefit in a not so smoothly running society because it is better than the Hobbesian chaos of being outside of society.

But even if you realize that taxes are a necessary evil that you willingly (if sullenly) submit to in order to be a part of a greater society, your subjective sense of fairness antennas are up to make sure that others in the society are paying their taxes fairly. But how you define fair depends on your specific circumstances. If you are a rich person you might think a highly progressive income tax is very unfair but a poor person would have the opposite view. Likewise the rich person might think a flat tax would be fair but the poor person would be very upset with such a tax.

Because of the subjective nature of fairness, fairness is not a good standard to use in establishing tax policy. The standard I prefer is the "not too unfair" standard. We might not be able to agree on what's fair but we should be able to come up with a tax policy that everyone can say (somewhat grudgingly) is not too unfair (although their objections might be for different reasons depending on a person's specific circumstances). The process of judging if a policy is not too unfair engages the rational brain and let's us control the instinctual brain that is screaming, "not fair, not fair!"

When President Trump announces his new tax proposal in a few weeks he will, no doubt, assert that it is very fair. Whole bunches of people across the country will wail that it is not fair. Of course it will be unfair. But will it be too unfair? In other words, will the majority of the population concede that despite its demerits, the tax policy's unfairness is outweighed by its benefits to society? That is the essence of the "not too unfair" standard.

But we must take care. The "not too unfair" standard requires a concession from all sectors of society. Keeping in mind that most of our recent national elections have only been won by a few percentage points, a policy that is supported by a narrow majority but violently opposed by a large minority does not meet the "not too unfair" standard. This is why it is important that we agree of the purpose of taxation. If we cannot agree on the purposes to which our taxes will be applied, it will be impossible to reach any sort of consensus on what the actual policy should accomplish.

The Obligation of Citizenship

As noted above, it is difficult to reach a consensus on fairness if the specific circumstances of citizens are very different. If large numbers of citizens pay no tax, their specific circumstances will not only be different than those that pay taxes, they will be in opposition to those citizens. Under such circumstances it will be very difficult to reach a "not too unfair" consensus.

All citizens need to pay some tax even if the other benefits received from government by the lower income sectors of society outweigh the taxes they pay. All citizens need to share the pain of loss to the takings of the government by the use of coercive power. In this way the common citizenship of all participants in society is reinforced.

Tax Manipulation

Taxes are powerful incentives that can be used to manipulate human behavior. Harken back to Prospect Theory. Psychologically, taxes are losses and losses hurt much more than gains. Humans, under the marching orders of the instinctual brain, are greatly motivated to avoid taxes even if the tax savings are minimal or not in their best interests.

The mortgage interest deduction has been pushed by realtors (most of these tax incentives are supported by one special interest group or another) as a way to increase the number of people owning homes, which is considered a good thing for most people. But home ownership in Canada, which does not have mortgage interest deduction, is 67.6% while in the United States it is only 64.5%. On the other hand, the average home size in the US is about 11% more than Canada (2164 sq. ft. to 1948 sq. ft.). So it would appear that the mortgage interest deduction does not improve the percentage of home ownership but does increase the average size of homes purchased (this may be an example of another problem with using tax incentives to manipulate people's behavior – unintended consequences).

In order to promote plug-in electric vehicles, the government offers up to $7500 in tax credits for purchasing such vehicles (although the average credit is usually much less). This credit only partially offsets the high cost of such vehicles. The New York Times in 2012 estimated that the cost break-even between plug-in electric vehicles and standard vehicles is between 8.6 and 26.6 years, depending on the model. And, although the plug-in cars may not produce CO_2, the power plants that supply the electricity do so it may also take years before the higher carbon production processes of electric vehicles are offset. So the societal gains are marginal at best but the government has determined that it wants to promote these vehicles and that a tax incentive was the best way to do it.

But I don't mind if government wants to promote plug-in electric vehicles. Governments promote many technologies and industries and some of these promotions have been very successful. Lucrative mail carrying contracts help support the early development of airplanes. The government's DARPA program spawned the development of the Internet.

But I do object to the government using taxes as the primary incentive for all these promotions. The government is trying to manipulate the behavior of citizens by using Prospect Theory to influence our instinctual brains. Richard Thaler and Cass Sunstein wrote a book, *Nudge*, about all the wonderful ways the government can manipulate our behavior for our own good. But it is not the government's job to manipulate our behavior, but rather it is government's obligation to follow the will of the people. This subtle manipulation has the relationship between the government and its citizens backwards.

By eliminating all these tax incentives we will not only stop all this manipulation of the people, but we will clean up the tax code so that people can actually understand what the government is doing. If the government wants to promote plug-in electric vehicles then write a check. Give it to the purchaser. Oh, and by the way, get the authorization of

Congress for the appropriation and make sure the cost is included in the budget report.

In the next segment of our discussion we will look at the impact of taxes and tax cuts on economic performance. This is the Holy Grail of tax policy.

2018 Perspective. See my essay, Grading the GOP Tax Bill, December 22, 2017.

Principles of Taxation III

February 20, 2017
Victor C. Bolles

In this third essay on the basic principles for tax reform we look at how taxes affect economic growth and at how other factors such as the national debt can change how the economy reacts to tax reform.

Tax Cuts and Economic Growth

Economic growth is the Holy Grail of tax policy. However the relationship of tax policy and economic growth is complex and simplistic solutions like merely cutting taxes are unlikely to generate the long-term economic growth this country needs. I am not talking about economic growth in the second or third quarter of 2017. My son just got promoted to management at his company. I want economic growth that will support his career for the next thirty years. My grandkids are in elementary school. They won't even be joining the workforce for twenty years. We need the kind of economic growth that America experienced in the nineteenth century that propelled our country from an agricultural backwater to an industrial powerhouse.

But what worked back then won't work now. Alexander Hamilton espoused high tariffs (our principal source of tax revenue at the time) and protectionism of embryonic domestic industries at the dawn of the Industrial Revolution (plus a little industrial espionage). We need new solutions for the 21st century.

The mantra from Washington is tax cuts. Tax cuts will power economic growth. Economic growth will generate more tax revenues. More tax revenues will change the deficit to a surplus that will pay down the national debt of $20 trillion. The tax cuts will be phenomenal. The deficit reduction will be big league. Isn't life wonderful?

Let's put a little reality into the tax cut equation. Tax cuts are the flip side of the Keynesian coin's increased government spending. The idea is that cutting taxes (or increasing government spending) will put more money in the hands of people who will go out and spend it thereby generating economic growth. In the wake of the Great Recession, our government tried both tax cuts and increased spending. Just about all we got was a doubling of the national debt (it is impossible to prove that things would have been worse if they had not taken these steps). We do know that the tax rebates went into savings accounts and the excess cash in banks sat in reserves - unlent and unproductive.

Keynes theorized that if a government cut spending during a recession because of reduced tax revenue, the reduced spending would exacerbate the recession. He therefore recommended deficit spending during a recession but he also recommended surpluses after the recession was over in order avoid increases in the national debt which otherwise would ratchet up on every downturn. Politicians did not pay attention to the second half of Keynes' recommendation so we have had surpluses in only 5 of the last 50 years (although we have only had about 7 years of recession in the last 50 years according to Wikipedia).

Milton Friedman hypothesized that tax cuts or deficit spending that increased the national debt would not generate much economic growth because people would realize that the debt would have to be repaid at some time in the future and that would require more taxes or reduced spending motivating people to save for the future rather than spend now (the Paradox of Thrift).

Keynes theory seems to work when government accounts are more or less in balance. And since the US economy is generally growing most of the time, the money required to reduce the debt accumulated during downturns would not be that much of a burden. But our politicians in Washington are loath to be seen restraining the economy in any way so long as even one person is unemployed, even if the purpose of this restraint is to reduce the national debt.

And so our national debt has continued to grow inexorably until it has now become a huge threat to our economy. As the national debt grows, Keynes' theory becomes less relevant and Friedman's becomes more relevant. As a result tax cuts and deficit spending do not work well when there is a large amount of national debt.

As fiscal policy has less impact when there is a large overhang of debt, so the effectiveness of monetary policy is also reduced. Like government spending and tax cuts, zero interest rates and quantitative easing are designed to put money in people's hands in order to induce them to spend more and generate economic growth. But all of the money pushed out into the economy has sat idle while the economy bumps along with sub-two percent growth.

The conundrum we face is not a contest between the theories of Keynes and Friedman/Hayek. It is a contest between the theories of Keynes and Kahneman. As the national debt grows the likelihood of a major financial crisis also grows. This was clearly demonstrated by Carmen M. Reinhart and Kenneth S. Rogoff in their book, *This Time Is Different: Eight Centuries of Financial Folly*. The chance of financial crisis increases as debt increases, especially after the national debt exceeds about 70% of GDP. The impact of such financial crises is much greater than what we experienced during the Great Recession (I know. I lived in Mexico during the Lost Decade after a financial crisis in 1981.). As we learned in our earlier essays on Kahneman's Prospect Theory, loss aversion means the fear of loss can overwhelm the hope of gain and as the national debt increasingly looms over the economy the fear of loss grows exponentially.

Obviously, not all citizens are familiar with these economic and psychological theories but there has been a pervasive feeling of unease in our country. A recent Rasmussen Report stated that 64% of the people in the country believed we are headed in the wrong direction. It is not our rational brain that understands economic theory behind this unease; it is our instinctual brain that raises the hair on the back of our collective necks.

And we must keep in mind the fact that the size of our national debt is dwarfed by the unfunded future obligations of Social Security and Medicare. The net present value of those future obligations has been estimated to be as much as $40-60 trillion. Many of our children and grandchildren don't believe they will ever see a benefit from these programs. That's some legacy we are leaving to our offspring.

Competitive Taxation

Many proponents of tax reform believe that the US corporate tax is too high and makes US businesses less competitive than their international competitors. The US corporate tax is near the top of those of developed countries. Further, the US is practically the only country to tax global income rather than only the income earned domestically. This uncompetitive corporate tax and its global scope have distorted how US companies do international business.

As a business grows it begins to export its products to other countries. As these markets grow, it may make good business sense to begin to have some operations located in the overseas markets. There are many reasons why a business may want to have some of its operations overseas. Some businesses have taken advantage of lower wages overseas to relocate their manufacturing plants to other countries and importing their products back into the United States (offshoring).

The profits from these operations are taxed at the rate in the foreign country, which is usually less than that of the US. The US does not levy the global tax on these earnings until the profits are repatriated back to the US. This has caused many companies to keep their foreign profits offshore. The amount of unrepatriated profits is estimated to be around $2 trillion. So instead of this money being reinvested in the United States is sits idle overseas or (worse) is reinvested overseas generating even more foreign profits (and more foreign jobs).

Some companies have even gone so far as to change their domicile from the US to a low-tax foreign country through a reverse merger (these transactions are called inversions) because it is so much more profitable to be a foreign company. The Obama administration concocted a huge penalty to thwart the proposed inversion of US pharmaceutical giant Pfizer but did not address the poorly conceived tax policy that prompted Pfizer to attempt the inversion in the first place.

Because US companies compete internationally they need a tax policy that does not impair their ability to compete. Some progressives may baulk at lowering corporate tax rates but lower rates that help to improve the ability of American companies to compete would help generate more jobs in America and eliminating the global taxation would bring new investment funds back on shore. Corporate taxes only represent about 11% of federal government revenues so the cost of competitive corporate tax rates would not have a large impact (besides, a good case can be made that the cost of taxes is pushed onto us consumers anyway in higher priced products).

Border Adjustment Tax

One of the tax reform proposals being discussed is a border adjustment tax that would levy a tax on imports but not on exports. Because we don't know if this new tax will actually end up in the proposal let's not waste a lot of time on it right now. The only thing I would say at this time is that this tax would be perceived by our trading partners as a tariff and they are likely to react accordingly, which could trigger a devastating trade war that could severely damage the US economy.

Tax Stability

Currently, the US tax regimen is horribly complex and, even worse, it changes every year. These changes can be minor or major but compliance costs are exorbitant because not reflecting even a minor change in a tax filing can have major penalties and even jail time. These changes can arise from special deductions or subsidies (those K Street lobbyists have to justify the enormous fees they charge) or they may be ideologically oriented (as are some of the taxes and penalties in the Affordable Care Act).

Businesses facing an uncertain tax (or regulatory) environment will be hesitant to invest in new plant and equipment or to hire new employees. A simplified and stable tax regime would permit US businesses to grow and promote economic growth and jobs (although accountants and lawyers might be negatively affected).

Combined with the other essays on the principles of taxation, I think we now have a framework that can be used to analyze the benefits and drawbacks of President Trump's forthcoming tax proposal. Based on the principles we have discussed, we can see that tax policy in a vacuum is not likely to be as phenomenal as its promoters predict.

2018 Perspective. See my essay, Grading the GOP Tax Bill, December 22, 2017.

March 2017

2017: A Trumpian Year in Review

unbrandedcare

March 15, 2018
Victor C. Bolles

Well it looks like the unbranded American Health Care Act is dying that long drawn out death usually only seen in black and white movies. I call it unbranded because no one wants his name attached to it. So we aren't calling it Trumpcare, Ryancare or GOPcare as the Democrats are trying to do to assign the blame for this attempt to repeal and replace Obamacare.

The reason that both Obamacare and unbrandedcare are such disasters is that they are attempts to cover the gaps and flaws of healthcare in America without reforming the deeply flawed system underpinning these programs. If you look at the two worst performing sectors of our economy (education and healthcare – most money spent with mediocre results at best) you will see that these are the two sectors where the government is most involved. In spite of its good intentions to improve the scope and delivery of these services, the mediocre results and outrageous expense are the unintended consequences of government help (Ronald Reagan's nine most terrifying words "I'm from the government and I'm here to help".)

Most of the interest in reforming healthcare is focused on its microeconomic impact: how it affects a person's ability to receive and pay for good healthcare. In this essay, however, I would like to focus on the macroeconomic impact of our healthcare system. In the US, 17% of Gross Domestic Product is spent on healthcare and medicines. This is far more than any other country. France, Switzerland, Japan, Germany and Sweden spend about 11% of the GDP on healthcare yet their citizens on average live two to five years longer than ours do. This means that 6% of our economy is absolutely wasted and worthless. We get nothing for it. Oh, by the way. That 6% is over a trillion dollars. Every year. Thrown away. Completely wasted.

Worse than that! Healthcare is sapping the strength and productivity of our economy. Healthcare to our nation is like maintenance in a factory. Both healthcare and maintenance are necessary to keep a nation and a factory running. So our factory owner spends money to keep his machines running and his building safe and sound. But maintenance is preventive. It is a cost. If maintenance costs are too high the factory will lose money and eventually shut down. Like maintenance, healthcare keeps our people healthy and productive. But it is a cost.

It is true that the government is heavily involved in healthcare in many countries and completely run by the governments of France, Germany and others. So why shouldn't the US also have a government run healthcare system? Would it be healthful and efficient? Maybe it would if we could get the Germans to come over and run it for us. Otherwise we might get a healthcare system more akin to the Veterans Affairs (VA) health system.

I suppose that we could try and emulate our European friends and design a government run healthcare system like the ones in France or Germany (don't do one like in the UK which is going broke). That is what both Republicans and Democrats are trying to do. How they want to do it differs (Democrats want to tax the one percent/Republicans want to give tax credits) but they both want the same thing. A healthcare entitlement for every citizen that wants one (and even for those that don't want one). I guess Joe Kernan was right when he said on CNBC that "you can't take an entitlement away." But this is the insidious nature of entitlements; they just keep growing and growing until they swallow up everything.

Or we could try something different. We didn't become the greatest nation on earth by being like everyone else. The free market economic system powered us on this rise to greatness but it is the one thing that is lacking in all these healthcare proposals.

Not being a healthcare expert, I can't tell you exactly how to structure this new healthcare system. But being an economic expert I can tell you some of the elements that need to be included in the plan so that the free market economic system can work its magic.

Some Republicans want to repeal and replace Obamacare right away. Some of the more reasonable Republicans say there needs to be a transition period that could last a year or two. But it took us generations to get in this mess and it will take a generation to get us out of this hole.

We need to make people pay for their own healthcare. However, in order to do this we need to make healthcare affordable. Making people pay for their healthcare will bring competition back into the system that will drive down prices – eventually. To do this immediately or even quickly would be impossible. Many people are fully invested in the current system and a rapid shift would leave them dangerously exposed. Today's retirees have paid a lifetime of taxes into Medicare and have no way to seek an alternative. We need to honor that obligation while making younger people begin to pay for their healthcare so that when they also retire they will be prepared.

We need to get rid of the double tax benefit for employer provided insurance. This tax benefit is one of the principal causes of the screwed-up mess that is healthcare in the US. Also, it doesn't match the structure of 21st century employment. Gone are the days when you walk into the factory door at eighteen (or older if a college grad) and walk out when you are sixty-five. Today's worker can be an independent contractor, part-timer, freelancer, self-employed or other variation. People need their own portable health insurance that goes where they go. If an employer wants to cover that cost as a benefit that's fine. But don't force it.

We need to solve the problem of pre-existing conditions, which was a major problem before Obamacare. I can think of several possible solutions so this is a problem that can be resolved in the marketplace. Having portable insurance will also stop people from being trapped with their current employer because currently changing jobs means changing insurance companies.

If oil sells all around the world at the same price (as does gold, silver, copper and many, many other things on the market) then why the hell are drug prices different in every country. Oh, I know the story. In these countries the government buys all the drugs so it can negotiate a sweetheart deal. The marginal production cost of drugs is minimal, the real cost is in research and development. So drug companies can sell cheap drugs at a profit in those countries as long as they can increase their prices in the US to cover their R&D. All those countries are freeloading off of us and that has to stop. That is something the government can do to help control healthcare costs, the companies can't do this on their own.

Once we get the free market economic system working in our healthcare system we will be able to get the cost of healthcare as a percent of GDP back down to earth and people will be able to afford their healthcare. Then we can get the health insurance companies back in the insurance business instead of being a big costly and inefficient payments system. Healthcare administrative costs in the US are the highest in the world (between 25 and 31 per cent according to several studies). That alone would equal the extra burden on our economy noted above. And administration isn't healthcare its just pushing paper and complying with government mandates.

So if Congress and President Trump want to get together and really provide us with a good healthcare system they should include these free market ideas in their plan.

2018 Perspective: Congress was unable to repeal and replace Obamacare although they have been able to rescind certain aspects of it such as the personal mandate. I believe this slapdash approach will make healthcare in the United States even more economically unsustainable.

I Dream of Gini

March 22, 2017
Victor C. Bolles

I just wanted to write this review of a book I recently read in order to save the reader from having to plow through this mind-numbing tome crammed with Gini coefficients from various historical periods for which it is impossible to calculate Gini coefficients. What are Gini coefficients you might ask? Wait a minute. First, I want to say that this is an important book. Not for what it says but for what it doesn't say.

The Great Leveler, Violence and the History of Inequality from the Stone Age to the Twenty-First Century (the title gives you a taste of what you are getting yourself into if you choose to read this book), by Walter Scheidel, tracks income and wealth inequality throughout the ages. It is an intriguing concept. How has wealth and income been apportioned by all the different societies and empires in the history of our world?

Professor Scheidel uses numerous methodologies to estimate the Gini coefficients of various historical societies and even pre-historic society. A Gini coefficient is a measure of statistical dispersion first published by Corrado Gini in 1912. A Gini coefficient of zero (0.00) would indicate that all values in the study are identical (for example, all the people have the same salary). A Gini coefficient of one (1.00) would indicate perfect inequality (for example, one person would have all the salary and the rest none). Economists use Gini coefficients to measure inequality of income or wealth distribution of countries (the World Bank publishes an annual study of Gini coefficients or you can look it up on Wikipedia).

In the real world it is impossible for wealth or income to have coefficients of one or zero or even come real close to such results. Globally, Gini coefficients for income after tax and transfers range from .20s to .60s with Norway one of the lowest at .259 and Haiti one of the highest at .608. Norway was recently voted the happiest country on Earth and Haiti, as we all know, is one of the most miserable places. Does this mean that income inequality is associated with dissatisfaction? Not necessarily. The US has a relatively high Gini at .411 while Niger at .310 is not so nice. Some of the most miserable countries (such as North Korea) don't report their economic performance so we have no idea of their income inequality.

Reliable economic information doesn't exist for many countries and ancient empires so Prof. Scheidel had to look for other data to reconstruct Gini coefficients in order to discern historical patterns. He spends a great deal of the book illustrating his calculation methodologies for various eras and countries, which is necessary to support his principal finding. His conclusion was that in virtually every period and country income inequality tends to increase over time. He further found that most attempts to reverse or reform this tendency were, at best, partial and always temporary.

The only way to significantly alter income distribution he found was through catastrophic events such as plagues or major wars that decimated the population. This decimation, such as the Black Plague that killed an estimated 30-60% of the population of Europe, requires a restructuring of society in order to adapt to the new conditions. But even with these catastrophic events, income inequality returned over time.

The last great catastrophe that reduced income inequality was in the early part of the twentieth century when two world wars plus the Great Depression (along with the communist revolutions in Russia and China) caused a significant reordering of society and a reduction in income inequality. This Great Compression, which began in the 40s, ran until the 1970s. Progressives look to this period as a time of rapid growth while income inequality was low due to highly progressive tax rates and New Deal redistribution policies. They use this period to justify their call for evermore redistribution programs and benefits along with high taxes to reduce income inequality.

But it is not just the left that looks to the fifties with nostalgia. This is the great period that President Trump wants to resurrect in his campaign promise to Make America Great Again.

But the Great Compression is a statistical anomaly. It was doomed to be temporary. Prof. Scheidel's investigation shows that income inequality has been increasing across the globe since the 1980s. Although high taxes and a substantial social welfare system have slowed this decompression in Europe there are indications of increasing income inequality there because rising debt has required cutbacks in some benefits (so progressives are deluding themselves if they think that their policy recommendations actually caused the Great Compression). The rapid economic growth of China has skewed the global totals because China's switch to state capitalism has caused the Gini in China to go from .230 not long after Mao's death to around .550 now.

Now we must go from the reporting historic economic trends to explaining why these economic trends occurred and what this means going forward. As foraging nomads, our ancient ancestors had little income or wealth inequality because they had little wealth or income at all. Wealth could only be accumulated once our ancestors settled down to farming about ten thousand years ago. Farming allowed the creation of surplus (also known as profit) and wealth accrued to those that controlled the land. But wealth rooted in land could be expropriated by the powerful so some of the men in the community had to specialize in protecting the land and in warfare instead of farming. This specialization as well as the creation of other trades to support the farmers led to the rise of classes among the people and to an unequal distribution of surplus. Surplus was the generator of economic growth but was also the creator of income inequality. This was why the Chinese communists adopted state capitalism to power economic growth that Mao's communism could not produce. They had to decide if they wanted to be communist and poor or capitalist and rich. Because poor also meant weak, they decided to be rich and strong.

Catastrophes, plagues and wars level the field because they eliminate surplus: capital goods and human capital. But what the book doesn't address is the Chinese question. Is it better to be equal and poor or unequal and rich? Poor people of today are infinitely better off materially than even the elites of times past.

Prof. Scheidel goes on to contemplate the type of progressive policies that would create less income inequality such as highly progressive taxes on the rich, confiscatory estate taxes and other measures to provide funds for transfer payments to equalize incomes. He even mused that nuclear conflict (to the extent it didn't wipe out the human race) would greatly reduce inequality. But he doesn't address the issue of why he thinks we should reduce income inequality.

Is income equality that important that all other aspects of human life must be sacrificed in order to obtain this equality? Prof. Scheidel stated clearly at the beginning of his book, "...economic growth requires some degree of inequality in income and consumption to encourage innovation and surplus production."

The only way to accomplish the dubious goal of income equality is to give more and more power to the state. Communists and socialists would assert that the surplus produced by the masses and appropriated by the state would be able to provide the economic growth the same as a capitalist system. But the state is not an economic animal. It is a political animal. And the goal of the state is not profit or economic growth but continuance in power. And the innovation and technological advancement that drives economic growth is a disruptor of an orderly (and well controlled) society. Therefore, surplus in communist/socialist economies is directed toward increasing the power of the state and innovation and progress are discouraged.

The civilization we live in, as unequal as it might be, is the culmination of 10,000 years of progress powered by surplus. It is the motivation to create and accumulate surplus that causes the inequality of income and wealth but it is also what has provided all this progress. Would it have been better that we remained wandering across the tundra in search of our next meal?

2018 Perspective: In my June 28, 2018 blog (Adios Horatio Alger) that cited an article by John F. Early of the Cato Institute (Reassessing the Facts about Inequality, Poverty and Redistribution), which noted that most countries do not include transfer payments when calculating Gini coefficients and that when these payments are included the income inequality is greatly reduced.

April 2017

The Opioid Economy

April 6, 2017
Victor C. Bolles

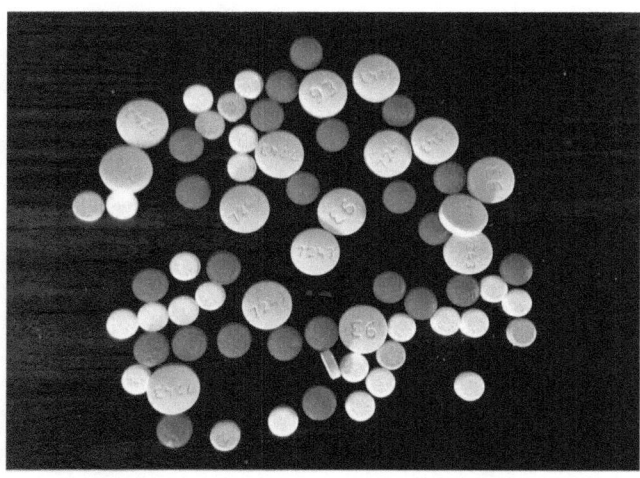

T
This morning on CNBC, Joe Kernan pounded his interviewees on the need for massive tax cuts to stimulate the economy. He excoriated the talking head money managers about the need to drop the corporate tax from the current 35 percent to twenty percent (as described in Speaker Paul Ryan's Better Way proposal) or even to fifteen percent as promised by then-candidate Trump on the campaign trail. When one of the talking heads (there are so many its hard to keep track all of them) had the temerity to suggest raising the top individual rate from 39% to 45% to offset reduced corporate taxes, Joe was apoplectic. He insisted we need massive tax

cuts to stimulate the economy no matter what it might do the deficit and the public debt.

If you have read any of my previous essays on taxes, you will already know that I am unconvinced that low taxes can do much more than provide a temporary burst of economic activity offset by the higher risk exposure of increased debt. Increased economic growth from the famous Reagan tax cuts was insufficient to absorb increased deficits and mounting debt, which rose from $1.5 trillion in 1982 to $6.4 trillion by 1997. Even John Maynard Keynes knows that if GDP increases from $3.3 trillion (in 1982) to $8.6 trillion (in 1997) you shouldn't have to increase debt by over 300%.

But then I thought, wait a minute! Why are we trying to stimulate economic growth by putting more money in the hands of corporations (something the Fed has been trying to do for eight years) when CEOs state that the biggest constraint to expansion is a lack of qualified workers? The Society of Human Resources Management says this is the most challenging market for finding talent in years. Today's stock market took off when ADP and Moody Analytics announced that private sector employment grew by 263,000. The Dow just recently broke 20,000 and is still near all-time highs. Why do we need more stimulus?

The Fed believes that the economy is strong enough that it can tighten its accommodative posture by raising short term interest rates two or three times this year. In addition the Fed is planning to start reducing the size of its balance sheet, which ballooned to $4.5 trillion in a largely futile effort to boost growth.

So why the heck is everybody so hell bent on further stimulating an economy that is already hitting capacity constraints? Are we addicted to stimulus?

Hitting capacity constraints at 2.0-2.5 percent growth means that there are structural issues in the economy that need to be addressed before we can begin to grow at a more rapid rate. These structural issues include things like the regulatory environment (including financial, environmental and healthcare regulation), crumbling infrastructure and an unmotivated and untrained workforce (not to mention an unsustainable social welfare system).

The structural issues also include a complex and opaque tax system that drags down business activity. But the structure of our tax system and the level of taxation are two different issues. A tax reform can be revenue neutral and still provide substantial reform. Some might say, if it doesn't lower my taxes why should I care about tax reform? If I can get you to overlook your own self-interest for a minute and try and see how the current tax system puts enormous burdens on our productive capacity you will understand how a thorough revision of how tax is calculated and collected would provide an enormous benefit to everyone even if the overall level of taxation remained the same.

Think of the countless hours expended on tax compliance by business owners and their tax advisors. Think of all the tortured and convoluted mergers and acquisitions that make little business sense but that provide enormous tax benefits. Think of all the innovation that could be generated when management is not bogged down filling out tax forms. And keep in mind that this tax system is more burdensome on small businesses (the ones that generate most of the employment in the US) that lack the resources of large corporations.

A reform to substantially reduce the complexity of the current tax code would have the additional benefit of providing greater transparency for the common citizen. Most people feel the tax system is loaded against them. This feeling is exacerbated by the opaqueness of the current tax code, reinforcing the lack of trust in government that is prevalent today.

The principal hurdle to a tax package is how to pay for the tax cut. Without the repeal of Obamacare the Republicans lack the funds to pay for their huge tax cuts (which also deprives the Democrats the opportunity to feign outrage at cutting off people's health coverage in order to give tax breaks to the wealthy). Once tax cuts are off the table, Congress can focus on cutting out all the subsidies and tax breaks that make our tax code such a mess. There will wailing and the gnashing of teeth from the corporate CEOs and their lobbyists as they try and preserve their treasured benefits that aren't available to the rest of us. The government gives away about $1 trillion in annual revenue because of all these subsidies and tax breaks. Cutting those subsidies out might leave enough room to have a little tax cut left over for the rest of us.

Through booms and busts we have had fiscal deficits in 45 of the last 50 years. It is time we go cold turkey on our addiction to stimulus!

2018 Perspective: Well we got the huge tax cut and the massive deficits that it will create. The economy is booming (more due in my opinion to deregulation than tax cut) and unemployment is at record low levels. Wonderful! We are already getting supply bottlenecks (exacerbated by new tariffs) and employers say they can't find people with the necessary skills to hire. So why is the Trump administration talking about more tax cuts?

The Weight of the World

April 10, 2017
Victor C. Bolles

It appears that President Donald Trump is beginning to realize the gravity and importance of the responsibilities placed on him as Commander-in-Chief of the United States. As leader of the free world he could not stand by and allow the heinous act of killing almost one hundred people in a sarin gas attack by the Syrian government go unpunished. He chose a missile strike on the airbase that was the launching point of the gas attack as the mechanism to punish the Assad regime for its horrible breach of human rights.

The gas attack was also a breach of the 2013 agreement between Russia and the US to eliminate weapons of mass destruction from the Syrian conflict. Then-president Obama had opted for a diplomatic agreement in lieu of military action. But diplomatic solutions only work when the parties to the agreement are acting in good faith (or compulsion). When working with counterparties like Assad, Putin and Khamenei good faith is hard to come by. President Trump's missile strike sends a message to the thugs around the world that there is a new marshal in town. It was an interesting juxtaposition that the strike took place while President Trump was meeting with President Xi of China. Without having to say a word, Xi got the message about North Korea.

Although the Trump administration has begun with fits and starts, miscalculations and downright boners, a pattern is beginning to emerge. They say that the responsibility of being president changes a man (or a woman in the future). Are we beginning to see President Trump acting presidential (if we can just get him to stay off Twitter)?

The TV pundits point to all the false starts and personnel changes in these early days of the Trump administration. It may be that the initial personnel of his administration were derived largely from the campaign and from people he knew in the business world. The appointment of Steve Bannon to the National Security Council presaged a more political focus on intelligence but his recent removal has allowed General McMaster to assume his proper role overseeing intelligence.

The Washington Post has highlighted some of the political infighting in the White house as the administration shifts from campaigning to governing. Some of the campaign-based rhetoric has also been shifting. Building the wall on the southern border is still a priority but it looks like the American taxpayer will be paying for it (at least initially). And it looks like NAFTA is going to be renegotiated rather than dumped. NAFTA is outdated. It was signed before there was an Internet or World Wide Web. At the very least it needs to be brought into the 21st century. But President Trump is probably learning in his meetings with CEOs that the US/Mexico supply chain is so thoroughly interdependent that simplistic solutions just won't work. I wouldn't be surprised if the Trans-Pacific Partnership makes a come back as it is now apparent that this was more a multilevel response to China than a simple trade agreement.

President Trump's discourse is still wrangles the ear. And many of his opponents wouldn't listen to a word he said even if he gave a speech worthy of Winston Churchill. And I don't doubt there are many missteps and personnel changes yet to come. But he does appear to be learning. Learning not how to appear to be presidential but to actually be presidential.

We are not out of the woods yet. But I do discern some small glints of light through the impenetrable forest. Now if someone would just take away his smart phone. How 'bout it, Ivanka?

Additional comment: The Syrian missile strike also highlights America's special position in the world. Many people scoff at the concept of American exceptionalism. Even President Trump has derided American globalism in his push for America First. During the campaign he was quoted as saying, "we have to stop being the policemen of the world."

But truth be told, no other nation or international organization could have done what the United States just did. Germany and France are not inclined to act (although France has taken decisive action on occasion in their former African colonies). The United Nations couldn't even issue a condemnation of the act. Russia and China seek to overthrow the western world order not to preserve and protect it. And Turkey is too busy stifling its democracy to take principled action. No, only the United States has the moral authority and military power to punish this evil act. The world has been waiting anxiously for America to put back on the mantle of leadership. All of us have learned over the last eight years that when the United States does not take the lead, bad things begin to happen. The role of world leader will require us to sacrifice our blood and treasure. This was something candidate Trump did not want to do. But this isn't about winning, it's about leading.

2018 Perspective: The mantle of global leadership lies like so much dirty laundry on the White House floor. After a promising meeting with North Korean dictator Kim Jung Il President Trump had a disastrous series of meetings with NATO leaders, UK Prime Minister May and Russian President Putin. President Trump's erratic policy shifts have unnerved allies and enemies alike, as he seems hell-bent on destroying the Pax Americana that has existed since the end of World War Two.

Our Jackie

April 19, 2017
Victor C. Bolles

The other day I was doing some chores while half listening to the TV. The presenters were doing a feature on Jackie Robinson who had been called up to the majors 70 years ago (April 15, 1947) to break the color barrier. The reporter interviewed a lady who stated she was so very proud that "he was one of ours." Believing she was referring to African-Americans, I thought to myself, "no, he was one of ours" meaning all Americans.

But then I realized that I had not only assumed that the woman had suffered from an us-versus-them mentality but that I had also done so by presuming what her response meant. Perhaps she had intended to include all Americans in her "ours". I went to the TV and ran back the DVR (how did I survive without that device) to see if I had been mistaken. This time I gave the piece my full attention but I could not find any indication of what she was thinking was included in her "ours'.

It may have been likely that she had, indeed, intended to only include African-Americans in her exclusive group of "ours" but we will never know. But it was my reaction that I was concerned about. Given the heightened racial tension that has developed in recent years despite the gains since the Civil Rights Movement, many blacks believe persistent discrimination still exists.

The experiences of South Carolina Senator Tim Scott were a revelation to me. On the Senate floor Scott, who is black, related his many instances of discrimination. One telling example was when he said he had been pulled over by the police five times in a year. I haven't been pulled over for so long that I do not remember when the last time was (I do remember the car I was driving –Isuzu Trooper -but that was many cars ago).

In my case, I was able to catch myself in my reflexive, instinctual thinking. It is our instinctual brain that reacts quickly to stimuli. For primitive humans, this was a vital attribute to have in order to survive in dangerous pre-historic conditions. But the instinctual brain can lead us astray in our more civilized times. Luckily for me I was able to engage my rational brain to sort out the flaws of my instinctual thinking.

We are living in irrational times. If you don't believe me, just read the comments section on any controversial news story. Discussion quickly degenerates to name calling and epithets. It doesn't matter if you are left-wing or right-wing, Democrat or Republican, progressive or conservative. The ability to have a reasonable discussion is almost impossible. Conservative speakers fear for their lives on many college campuses. Whether it is a rally in support of President Trump or a protest against him, there will be cadres of counter-protestors itching for a fight.

Most economic theories assume that people make rational economic decisions. However, behavioral economists such as Daniel Kahneman and Amos Tversky have shown that many economic decisions are not rational but instinctual (which is why there are no one-handed economists). Likewise, democracy is dependent on having a rational citizenry in order to function properly. Unfortunately, as in economics, people often react to their gut feelings over their rational brains. Politics and economics are so closely intertwined it is hard to separate where one ends and the other begins so Kahneman's theory applies to both equally.

Is there no way to stop ourselves as we sink down into irrational populism? How do we stop ourselves from tribal identification of people who share the same racial, religious or class characteristics? Hate of the opposition builds the cohesion of the group as noted by Psychiatrist Anna Fels in her New York Times opinion piece, the Point of Hate (April 14, 2017). And social media provides a feedback loop that reinforces our pre-set convictions without the interference of rational discussion.

All of this fermenting hate is metastasizing into our daily life; determining the movies we see and the chicken sandwiches we buy by their political purity. The American

Social Contract is crumbling before our eyes and seeping through our hands like so many grains of sand.

The crumbling of our social contract has been aided and abetted by our elected leaders, corporate elites and self-serving community organizers that have tried to capture the American democratic experiment for their private interests. The black community has particularly been subjected to the disadvantages of this unlevel playing field but other groups also suffer from a lack of equality of opportunity. The erosion of the social contract creates disillusion among the citizenry who are then vulnerable to the siren song of populism of both the left and the right.

But populism believes in outcomes, not processes. The only way to achieve the desired outcomes regardless of the social or economic inputs is through the coercive power of the state. Populism inevitably devolves into authoritarianism. Following such a path dooms our children and grandchildren to decades, if not generations, of impoverished tyranny.

Jackie Robinson came from a generation that believed that they could make a better world. Jackie's move to the majors and his subsequent career was a step toward that better world. That woman on TV was the beneficiary of the actions of Jackie Robinson and many others. The only hope for a brighter future is through reinvigoration of and propagation of our western values by re-engaging our rational brains through our individual actions as exemplified by Jackie Robinson. Jackie Robinson was one of ours.

2018 Perspective: The situation is palpably worse in 2018 than in 2017. As Amy Chua noted in her article in Foreign Affairs magazine, *Tribal World* (July/August 2018), and also in her recent book Political Tribes (2018), populism on both the left and right is appealing to the tribal nature of humans. The identity politics of the left is clearly trying to break America into various tribal identities. But President Trump is doing the same in urging blue-collar whites to Make America Great Again (like it was when whites were in charge).

Vive la Différence
April 25, 2017
Victor C. Bolles

The French election results are in and markets are celebrating the second place finish of the national Front's Marine Le Pen. Pundits are claiming that this election, along with the recent defeat of Gert Wilders in the Dutch elections, shows that the populist right's tide has turned and that the fate of social democratic Europe is assured, at least for the time being.

But it does not take a much deeper analysis to show that all is not right in French politics. The winner of the election, Emmanuel Macron, is a member of the French elite who has never held public office. He is the leader of a political movement, En Marche, which he founded in 2015 that has no deputies in the French National Assembly. His ability to govern, if elected, must be in doubt.

The traditional French political parties, the Republicans and the Socialists, suffered ignominious defeats, getting less than 20% for the Republican candidate and a pitiful 7% for the Socialists. But these two parties control over 82% of the seats in the National Assembly. What's going on?

The rejection of the mainstream parties is indicative of the general dissatisfaction in France, and much of the rest of Europe, with the perceived defects in the governance of the European Union and the impact it has on citizens. They see economic stagnation, high unemployment (especially among youth) and uncontrolled immigration as the principal causes of their dissatisfaction. The French feel they are losing the soul of their nation. Not the soul of Europe, but of the French nation. This is the same discontent that led to Brexit. This was the wave that Marine Le Pen rode to national prominence. And Gert Wilders. And others. This tide is not ebbing. One cannot tell if the receding wave means the tide has turned or if the next wave will advance even higher.

The European Union is very fragile. The British are leaving. Greece almost had to leave and is hanging on barely. The fate of the Euro as a currency is very uncertain. Europe is very much like America was under the Articles of Confederation, an agglomeration of different polities bound together with only the merest strands of commonality. The American colonies had one advantage the Europeans lack. Virginians felt that they were very different from Massachusettsans. But they all had a common British heritage (in those days most people – except slaves- came from Britain) and almost all spoke the same language. They had also banded together in a war of independence and had shared many sacrifices to achieve that independence.

When the Articles of Confederation proved to be inadequate for the new nation, the colonists were able to come together in the Constitutional Convention to hammer out a document to unite all the various colonies. It was not easy but it was possible.

Europeans lack these advantages. A Frenchman believes that he is French first and European second. The same for Germans. The same for Italians. They all speak different languages. It is very hard for them to reform the European Union to create a great nation state. In fact, some European states are beginning to break up into even smaller units. The Czechs separated from the Slovaks. The Catalonians and the Basques want to be separate from Spain. The Scots want to be separate from Great Britain.

The United States is also going through a period of dissatisfaction with the status quo. According the latest Rasmussen poll, 53% of the country thinks the United States is heading in the wrong direction (although this is a great improvement from last year when at one time 72% thought we were going in the wrong direction). But, despite some rumblings from ultra-liberal California, the United States is not about to break up.

I am American first and Texan (where I live) second. Neither am I a Michigander where I grew up and went to school (Go Blue!). Nor am I an Illini from where I was born. I am not a hyphenated American. Although I am proud of my heritage I am more concerned about where we are all going than where we are all from. I think most Americans would agree.

There is another important factor that our European friends lack. Although relatively few Americans now have the British heritage (or it is much attenuated) that bound the colonists together, we share a common philosophy. More than any other country, America was founded on a set of principles and it is those principles that bind us together in an edifice of trust. The current unhappiness on the direction of our country is not due to dissatisfaction with those principles but in the failure of our leaders to adhere to those principles.

Although Europeans participate in western culture, you cannot say that they share a common culture. Each culture (and subculture) is different. While the Europeans want to benefit from economic integration, they lack the will to take the necessary steps to forge a common culture. The electoral results have been in reaction to EU officials in Brussels trying to impose an administrative European culture over the traditional cultures of the various countries in the union. Economic integration is very different from cultural integration and the people of Europe are stating their preference for their local cultures.

There is an important lesson here for us Americans as well. Certain factions in this country (you know who they are) are trying to assert the moral equivalence of different cultures and to foist multiculturalism and multilingualism on Americans. But Europe is showing us that this is not the route to greater unity and harmony but a road disharmony and eventual break up. Only by adherence to our American principles based on western Enlightenment philosophy can we achieve the unity we seek so that we can put our country on the right course.

2018 Perspective: Little has changed in the intervening year. The Italian government was cobbled together by non-traditional parties (the League – previously the Northern League – and the Five Star Movement) and are considering ditching the Euro and contemplating a referendum on EU membership. The United States has not yet learned the lesson to be gained from watching the deterioration of Europe.

A Principled Analysis of the Trump Tax Reform Plan

April 27, 2017
Victor C. Bolles

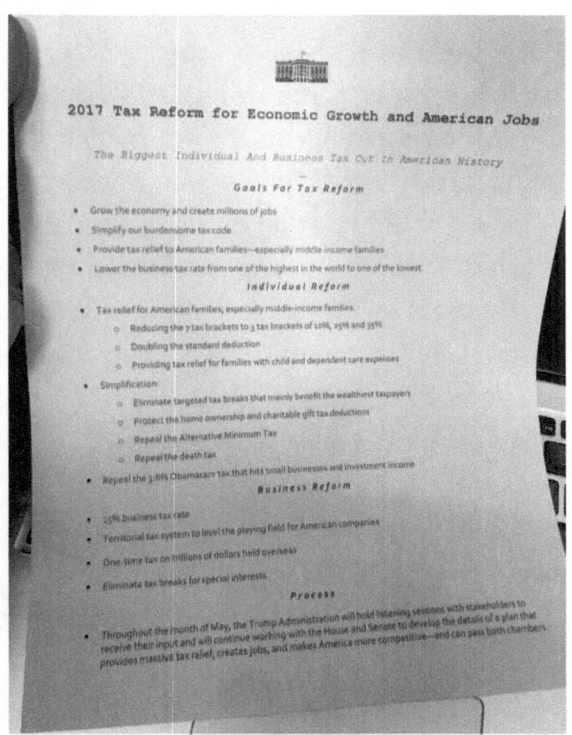

Okay. Chief Economic Adviser Gary Cohn and Treasury Secretary Steven Mnuchin have just released President Trump's much awaited tax reform plan. It is a single sheet of paper with 19 lines on the goals of tax reform and the proposals. This is what the administration has been working on so arduously for three months. It looks like something that you or I could come up with in a half an hour.

The devil is in the details and we have few details here. Of course, such a proposal can only be a bare outline because it has to go through the legislative process and many changes are likely during that process. We also do not have the scoring of the Congressional Budget Office on the likely impact of this package (as well as commentary from other economists who might disagree with the CBO figures).

But even in this rough cut form I think it is important to look at how this proposal fulfills the principles outlined in my recent essay, The Summation of the Principles of Taxation (a combination of the three previous essays on the Principles of Taxation, above). I will try to explain how these principles are addressed in such a manner that it makes sense even to those that have not read the Summation (and it might make you want to go back and take a look at it).

The Goals for Tax Reform

The plan's goals are:

- Grow the economy and create millions of jobs

- Simplify our burdensome tax code

- Provide tax relief to American families – especially middle-income families

- Lower the business tax rate from one of the highest in the world to one of the lowest

This is a very Keynesian tax proposal. It assumes that that lower taxes generates higher growth because it puts more money in the hands of the people who are supposed to go out and spend or invest it. This is the same concept used by the Democrats to justify increased government spending. Such policies might be warranted if we were in a recession (as was Keynes original concept) but we have had slow but steady growth for eight years, which has resulted in tight labor markets that cannot be closed because of a skills gap and other structural issues (of which the level of taxation is only one). It is hard to see how putting more money into an economy awash in money from deficit spending and quantitative easing is going to suddenly create faster growth. Further, a paper (On Charlatans and Cranks, July 2, 2007) on dynamic scoring by Matthew Weinzierl and Greg Mankiw estimated that a broad-based income tax cut (applying to both capital and labor income) would recoup only about a quarter of the lost tax revenue through supply-side growth effects. The result would be huge increase in the already huge public debt as also occurred after the Reagan tax cuts.

Individual Reform.
- Tax relief for American families, especially middle-income families:

- Reducing the 7 tax brackets to 3 tax brackets of 10%, 25% and 35%
- Doubling the standard deduction
- Providing tax relief for families with child and dependent care expenses

- Simplification
  - Eliminate targeted tax breaks that mainly benefit the wealthiest taxpayers
  - Protect the home ownership and charitable gift tax deductions
  - Repeal the Alternative Minimum Tax
  - Repeal the death tax

- Repeal the 3.8% Obamacare tax that hits small businesses and investment income

I don't see how a reduction in the number of brackets would substantially simplify the tax system. This was not really a problem even before computers and TurboTax. We have no idea at what income level these tax brackets apply so it is not possible to determine the impact of tax revenue or how much relief is provided to taxpayers. Doubling the standard deduction would provide a significant (and costly) benefit to lower and middle-income taxpayers. The standard deduction was the only deduction recommended in my original proposal because lower income taxpayers would have to forego necessities to pay for these taxes in the absence of the standard deduction compared to upper income taxpayers who would have to forego luxuries. This proposal would be deemed fair by a large segment of the population but because it affects so many taxpayers it will be very costly. I would prefer that child and dependent care expenses be handled directly through subsidy payments rather than through the tax system.

The elimination of tax breaks for the wealthy is a laudable goal but here we need to know exactly what tax breaks are being discussed. In my proposal I advocated eliminated all tax breaks. This would greatly simplify the tax system. If it was felt beneficial to offer benefits for certain actions by taxpayers (such as installing solar panels or buying an electric plug-in vehicle) these incentives could be provided by direct payments authorized by Congress rather than through the tax system. The same could be said for tax credit for lower income taxpayers as well. There are ways to provide these benefits without using the tax system. The manipulation of the behavior of the people through the use of tax incentives is a perversion of the limited role of government envisioned by the Founders.

The so-called home ownership deduction is actually a mortgage interest deduction. In my full essay I show that the mortgage interest deduction does not promote a higher percentage of home ownership but rather the purchase of larger homes subsidized by taxpayers. Lower and middle-income families do not pay enough mortgage interest to justify the use of the itemized deduction option so this benefit is primarily for the wealthy.

I know the charitable gift tax deduction is popular and it may be one of the reasons why Americans give so generously compared to other countries. But there may be better ways to achieve this worthy goal. I remember during the 2012 election campaign I read that Republican candidate Mitt Romney donated a substantial portion of his income to charity. He gave 29.4% of his $13.7 million income ($4.0 million) to charity. Wow! That's a lot. About 80% of Mr. Romney's gifts, however, are to the Mormon Church. If we substituted direct payments instead tax deduction as I have proposed for other deductions, the US government would have to write a multimillion-dollar check to the Mormon Church. I don't mean to pick on Mr. Romney (I just remember that fact from pervious research). Many people do this (mostly wealthy because of the itemized deduction thing). I just don't think a lot of people would support the government writing billions of dollars of checks to religious organizations but the tax deduction for charitable gifts has the exact same budgetary impact (although tax expenditures such as the charitable giving tax deduction are not included in the official budget).

Not mentioned on this brief sheet of paper but discussed in the press conferences was the elimination of the deduction for state and local taxes. This is a good idea. This deduction currently requires that the federal government subsidize tax-hungry progressive states like California at the expense of low-tax business friendly states like Texas. Whether you are progressive or conservative the federal government has no business subsidizing one state at the expense of another.

The Alternative Minimum Tax should have been repealed long ago. Period.

I have always felt that the Death Tax (actually the Estate Tax) is an unjust tax. It is a punitive tax on wealth, punishing people for being successful. It is onerous, placing a heavy burden on a grieving family that might have to sell the family estate or business in order to generate the funds to pay the tax. Furthermore, in many cases taxes have already been paid on the income that created the estate so that, in these instances, the estate tax is double taxation. A case could be made that the tax basis (book value) of the estate is far below the current market and that the inheritance of the estate is a financial transaction that requires the establishment of a new tax basis. But in these cases, the basis should be adjusted for inflation and be paid in installments (just like my long term capital loss carryover on a bad investment can only be $3,000 per year). On the other hand, a wealth tax on the value of an estate is not an unreasonable tax. Middle-income families pay property tax on their major wealth asset (their home) but wealthy families do not pay anything on their financial assets that represent a much larger portion of their wealth.

Repealing the 3.8% Obamacare tax before repealing Obamacare will leave the government with an unfunded expenses mandated by law. Without these funds, the size of the fiscal deficit will increase.

Business Reform

- 15% business tax rate

- Territorial tax system to level the playing field for American companies.

- One time tax on trillions of dollars held overseas

- Eliminate tax breaks for special interests.

One gets the feeling that the 15% corporate tax rate is an opening bid in a lengthy negotiation. That may be so. But the United States must be careful not to instigate a bidding war with other countries on who has the lowest rate. That will just beggar all the other developed economies. And, although most of corporate taxes are passed on to consumers in the form of higher prices, many people will feel that a 15% rate is a giveaway to rich fat cats who don't need a break. A better idea would be to go to the G-20 meeting of developed economies and establish a range of corporate rates so that one country's rates does not disrupt those of its neighbors and trading partners (of course in the private sector this would be an illegal collusion).

The global tax system of the United States has disrupted and distorted how our private sector does business and led to companies not only keeping foreign earnings offshore but also investing those offshore funds in operations that compete with the US. A switch to a territorial tax system would allow US companies to compete with the international competitors on a more even basis.

Likewise a one-time tax on repatriating offshore funds is a reasonable idea. Many people would consider a tax-free repatriation an unfair giveaway. So a one-time tax in combination with a switch to a territorial tax system is a good idea.

Businesses are taxed on the difference between revenues and expenses so deductions are a key part of business taxation. But the complexity of the tax code derives from special tax treatments for certain companies or industries (particular interests). Elimination of all these special treatments is a key element in developing a tax system that will be deemed not too unfair by the citizenry (a fair system being an unachievable goal).

Issues not addressed in the tax proposal.

- Capital gains tax: the gain should be taxed the same as other income but the amount of the gain should be adjusted for inflation.

- Dividend double taxation: dividends should be deductible by companies and taxed only on the recipient of the dividend.

- The double tax exemption of healthcare benefits: this double exemption has resulted in the distorted healthcare mess we currently have in the US. Again, the recipient of this benefit should pay the tax.

- Border tax: Although the Trump administration is leery of this new tax, House Republicans are counting on $1 trillion in taxes on imports over 10 years from this tax to cover the lower corporate tax rates. This is the equivalent of asking foreigners to pay for our tax cut. Don't expect our trading partners to sit idly by while we gouge them for all this money. Besides, Veronique de Rugy and Daniel J. Mitchell showed in a recent op-ed piece in the Wall Street Journal (The Border-Adjustment Sleight of Hand) that the playing field is already level.

Conclusion

Some elements of the Trump Administration tax proposal are good and some are not so good. If the administration and Congress can come up with a plan that achieves the proposal's stated goals they will have achieved a major piece of legislation. President Trump will be accused of feathering his own nest because some of the tax proposals would greatly benefit his business interests. People are demanding to see his tax returns in order to determine how he will benefit from these proposals. This is a legitimate request of a publicly elected official because it is the appearance of a conflict of interest that must be avoided.

It will be a while before we begin to see the details of this tax plan and also see how Congress begins to try and distort it. The Trump plan goes partway in clearing up the mess of confusing deductions and corporate welfare but it would be better if the plan made a clean break. Particular interests (which means not the public interest) are what drive the electoral cycle in Washington. Lobbyists try and get legislators to draft legislation (especially tax legislation) in the interest of their clients. Legislators need the support of the lobbyists in order to get reelected. While a partial solution to the tax code mess is better than nothing, it leaves space for K Street to try and insert some tax benefits for their clients. A clean break, as I proposed, would clear the field and expose such maneuvering to the light of day.

Don't sit back and wait to see what Congress comes up with. Let your congressional representative know how you feel.

2018 Perspective. See my essay, Grading the GOP Tax Bill, December 22, 2017.

May 2017

Windage

May 10, 2017
Victor C. Bolles

The Huffingtonpost reported in 2016 that only 6% of Americans trust the media. Journalists are incredulous! Why that is only a couple of percentage points better than that swamp, the US Congress. We are just reporters, they wail. We just call it like we see it. You can't blame us for what we are reporting.

The University of Indiana's School of Journalism reports that only 7% of journalists identify as Republicans (they probably all work for Fox News). Four times as many (28%) identify as Democrats. That's pretty overwhelming. But a whopping 50% identify as independents.

Independent? If they're so independent why do over 80% of them vote Democratic? Consistently since the 1960's. And what about the other 15% that report "other"? I doubt that they are voting Libertarian. Hell, even ESPN has been outed for liberal bias and political correctness. Man, when you mess with my sports you gonna be in trouble (ESPN lost 762,000 subscribers in the first quarter of 2017).

I believe that journalists truly believe that they are unbiased. They believe that moderate Republicans are right of center while moderate Democrats are centrists. They don't believe that Social Democratic Europe is left of American principles. Instead, they believe that the European social welfare state is what America should be if we were as enlightened as the Europeans.

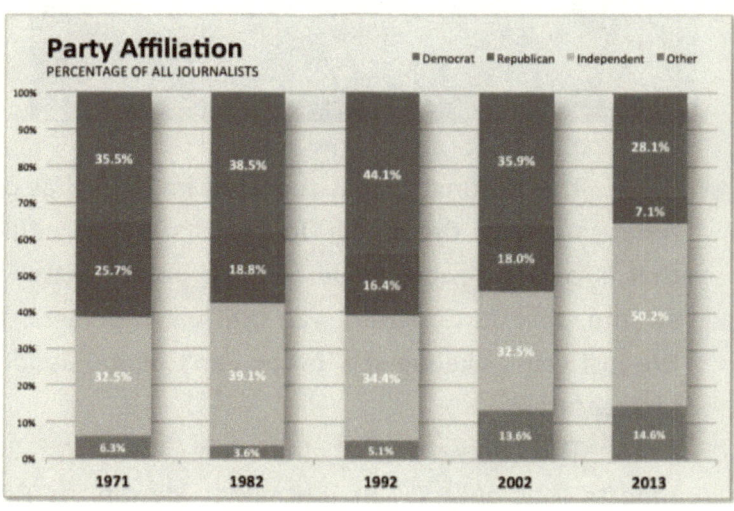

Indiana University, School of Journalism

2017: A Trumpian Year in Review

There is a left wind blowing in American newsrooms and citizens need to add some windage to their reporting to compensate for that bias. This left-of-center bias is not just in the newsroom. It is taking over political discourse all across the country. More and more people want more from the government. More healthcare, more education, more, more, more. More and better healthcare is a good thing. But if the cost is more government, isn't there a point where the government ceases to be our servant and becomes our master (if we haven't already passed that point)?

Americans are in danger of losing their essential freedoms (about which Ben Franklin warned us). Freedom is a rare thing. Throughout human history the vast majority of people have not been free. In ancient kingdoms, vast empires and modern dictatorships, the number of people that were free was ridiculously small. A fraction of a percent. Most people were slaves, serfs, peasants, helots or peons. They were bound to the land that they worked but did not own. Their survival was dependent on the good will of their lord and master.

You have to understand history in order to know how rare and precious freedom is. And fragile. The Germans lost their freedom when they voted for Adolf Hitler. The Italians lost their freedom when they chose Mussolini. The Venezuelans lost their freedom when they succumbed to Chavez' promises. Why did they do it? They wanted something. They wanted something and were willing to wager their freedom to get it. They lost that wager.

These people didn't lose their freedom to foreign aggressors. They lost their freedom to their own leaders. Leaders that they had selected.

Don't feel smug, my friend. Freedom is just as fragile in America as it was (and is) in those other countries. The 2016 presidential election shows just how fragile our precious freedoms are and highlights the danger they still face. The Democrats, led by Ms. Clinton and Mr. Sanders, espoused the "what works" philosophy of the left as described by Saul Alinsky in his book, *Rules for Radicals* (described as the bible of the left). Ms. Clinton actually wrote her senior thesis on Mr. Alinsky but turned down the job offer to work for him (by the way, former President Obama's job as a community organizer was for a group founded by Mr. Alinsky).

But President Trump also believes in the "what works" philosophy although I doubt he has read Mr. Alinsky's book (or much of anything else). He won by promising to use the coercive power of the state to provide vanished blue-collar jobs among other things. He would have probably promised to make the trains run on time if our railroads were as bad as Italy's were (Google it if you are confused). Populists believe in the use of state power just as much as leftists.

The problem is that Americans are electing leaders that promise to get them things. Things like free healthcare, free college education, and high-paying jobs that don't require any skill or experience. Our leaders state that these giveaways reflect American values and our media backs them up. They may reflect current American values but they don't reflect the values or principles on which America was founded, the most important of which were personal liberty and economic freedom.

2018 Perspective: In July of 2018 Democratic voters in the New York's privacy rejected veteran Congressman Joe Crowley in favor of Anastasia Ocasio-Cortez, an avowed socialist and campaigner for Bernie Sanders. As a member of the Democratic Socialists of America she endorses that party's positions of state ownership of industry and the elimination of profits. She naively believes that that socialism is democratic.

With Great Fanfare

May 22, 2017
Victor C. Bolles

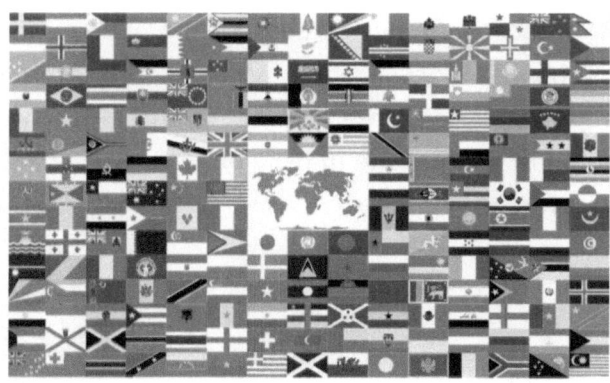

On his first overseas trip as President Donald Trump signed, with great fanfare, a $110 billion arms deal with Saudi Arabia. This bilateral deal with the oil kingdom is a clear win for the president. And President Trump likes to win. Of course, the deal had been in the works for years but had been blocked by the Obama administration. But still, a win is a win.

President Trump has stated that he much prefers bilateral trade deals over big, bulky multilateral pacts like the Trans-Pacific Partnership (TPP). One his first acts as president was to withdraw US participation from the TPP. Multilateral trade deals are messy, difficult agreements. The TPP negotiations lasted seven years and the still incomplete ratification process has been on-going for another year. The

Doha Round of trade negotiations comprising 159 countries began in 2001 and is not yet concluded.

It is hard to describe these big multilateral trade agreements as wins. Countries have to make many concessions in order to appease the concerns of the other countries. Each country has powerful domestic constituencies (and special interests) that must be placated. A win in one arena such as intellectual property may be offset by a concession in agricultural exports.

The reason President Trump prefers bilateral deals is likely an outgrowth of his years as a businessman and dealmaker. Dealmakers prefer one-on-one negotiations. Even in very complex transactions, many of the elements of the transaction are negotiated separately. You make one deal with your bankers. You make a separate deal with your investors. You have a different negotiation with the city or state on tax concessions. You cut a separate deal with the trade unions. When all the separate negotiations are assembled into the final transaction, nobody knows exactly what the dealmaker's cut will be.

Translating this experience into international trade deals will allow President Trump to use the size and power of the United States to overwhelm our trade partners, just like Mr. Trump did with his partners in his real estate deals. His business deal track record is littered with bankrupted partners, stiffed suppliers and sour grapes. No matter. Each one was a win for the Trump Organization. Those guys were a bunch of doofuses anyway.

A series of bilateral trade deals where the US dominates smaller countries may be notched as wins to bolster the self-esteem of the president, but they may not serve the long-term interests of the country. Multilateral trade deals may be difficult to negotiate. And they may be difficult to portray as clear victories. But multilateral trade deals are intended to be win/win collaborations not win/lose contests.

President Trump's purported goal in these bilateral trade deals is to reduce the US's enormous trade deficit. But the causes of the US trade deficit are more complex than just bad trade deals. First, the actual amount of the US trade deficit may much less than the reported amount. In an article in the in the Wall Street Journal (*The True Trade Deficit*, May 18, 2017) Brookings Institute analysts Martin Neil Baily and Adam Looney stated that US exports in 2012 were understated and that the "true" deficit was only $257 billion instead of the reported $537 billion. One reason for this undercounting is the $2.4 trillion in cash parked in offshore tax havens by US corporations because of the flawed tax policy of the US. The US fiscal deficit also drives up the trade deficit. There are other structural reasons such as the skills gap that are holding back US production and exports. And finally, forcefully reshoring US manufacturing will not create the high-paying manufacturing jobs President Trump's rustbelt supporters are longing for. Those jobs will go to robots, AI and the engineers and programmers that keep them running.

Placing the blame for the trade deficit on poorly negotiated trade deals is an oversimplification that will divert us from resolving the underlying structural problems. Renegotiating trade deals is unlikely to have a significant impact of the trade deficit but could possibly trigger a trade war that would create devastation across the globe that would dwarf the Great Recession.

But these international trade deals are important for another reason. Large multilateral trade deals, along with the World Trade Organization, set the rules for international trade. By agreeing to these rules, even if one particular rule does not work in our favor, we are establishing a rule of law for international trade. Not just with the transactions with us, but also in their transactions with each other. These trade partners are agreeing not just to specific trade terms but also to the concept of the rule of law, a concept that is one of basic building blocks of our democracy. By agreeing to transact business within the parameters outlined in these trade deals, they are agreeing to operate in conformance to how we envision the world should function.

So the Trans-Pacific Partnership was more than just a complex multilateral trade deal. It was an agreement by 12 countries on how the world should work. How we envision the world should work is different from how other countries might want the world to operate. President Xi of China is already attempting to claim the mantle of leadership in the area of world trade that the US has supposedly renounced. China's mercantilist vision of world trade is very different from ours. If they get to set the rules, it will be to our disadvantage. Not only to our trade balance, but to our standing in the world and our national security.

Among other things, TPP was intended to be a message to China that this is how we want international trade to function. If you want to trade with us you must follow our rules. China agreed to follow the rules when it joined the World Trade Organization but its mercantilist stratagems are not in alignment with WTO objectives. Enforcing WTO rules and demanding protection of our intellectual property rights will do more to rebalance our trade flows than renegotiating deals. And rejoining TPP along with a modernization of NAFTA terms would help insure that the terms of world trade continue to reflect the values and principles of America and our allies.

2018 Perspective: President Trump has determined that reducing the losses incurred by trade deficits are more valuable to the US than the system of alliances that have been the hallmark of the American led world order. In 2018 he launched an economic war not just on China but also on our allies. I don't see how this is going to help our economy or our security. Oh, by the way. After the Smoot-Hawley tariffs were imposed in 1930 resulting in a global trade war that caused the Great Depression, the United States had a trade surplus until World War Two. Something to look forward to.

June 2017

I Don't Want Your Damn Help, Al

June 1, 2017
Victor C. Bolles

photo by Matt H. Wade

This morning (Thursday, June 1, 2017) while promoting his new book on CNBC, Senator Al Franken (D-MN) said that being a senator was the best job he ever had because "you get to improve people's lives." He said he had been inspired by his mentor, the late Paul Wellstone, describing him as a great progressive, who stated that "politics is not about winning, not about money, but about improving people's lives".

Ignoring the fact that no one in America in their right mind believes that politics is not about money and winning, the statement that politics (and by implication government) is supposed to improve people's lives is patently false. As noted in a Wall Street Journal book review on the same day but on a different subject "the purpose of government was to secure the rights of life, liberty and the pursuit of happiness."

The purpose of government is to insure our freedom to pursue our own goals. This personal liberty is the engine that made America the richest, most powerful country on earth. Millions of Americans pursuing their own goals provides a wide, diverse generator of creativity. It is this creativity and innovation that has powered our economic and technological growth. It has also powered academia and the arts.

Now, you might not think that TV sit-coms are high art but not everyone travels the globe to see the latest rendition of Der Ring des Nibelungen as opera buffs are wont to do. But that is what diversity is all about. Sit-coms for Joe six-pack and the ring cycle for the literati. And a plethora of alternatives in between.

It is arrogance on the part of progressives to believe that they know best and that they can improve my life better than I can myself. They don't know what I need. They don't know what I want. In their fervor to control our lives for our own good they ban sugary drinks and raise the taxes on cigarettes to astronomical heights. They force me (and you) to purchase insurance for anatomically impossible medical procedures.

    I don't want you to improve my life into your left-wing vision of what my life should be. I have my own vision. I want my government to make sure I have the freedom to try to accomplish my vision my way. So, Al. Thanks but no thanks. I don't want your damn help.

    2018 Perspective. Al Franken no longer has "the best job he ever had." Hurray!

Heartless

June 23, 2017
Victor C. Bolles

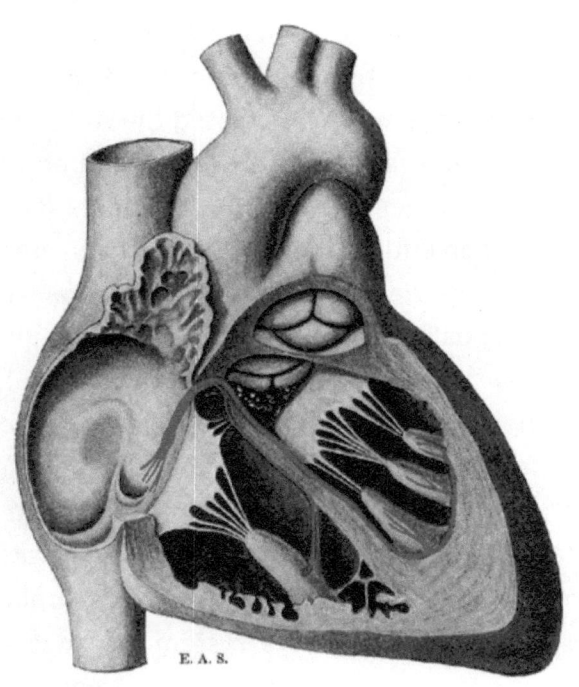

President Donald Trump had called the House's healthcare bill to replace the Affordable Care Act (Obamacare) "mean" and said he hoped that the Senate version would be a "plan with heart" (which he apparently equates with more money). Well, the Senate came out with their plan yesterday (June 22, 2017) and it took Senator

Chuck Schumer (D-NY) about ten seconds to label it "heartless". All I know is that if you are dependent on a kind-hearted government for your well being you are in deep trouble.

I don't need to read the wonkish details of the Senate's plan to know that it is basically an entitlement that they are trying to disguise as something else. It is likely to be a step back from the two or three steps forward that President Obama made when he created the Affordable Care Act. But it is still an expansion of the healthcare entitlement. As Charles Krauthammer said on Special Report (Fox News) "you can't retract an entitlement once it has been granted".

Thus the rage we witness as protestors against the bill proclaim that repealing Obamacare equals death (it makes me wonder how they survived prior to Obamacare). These people believe that they are totally dependent on government for their well-being and only a cruel, heartless government would take that away from them. And that is exactly what the progressive wing of the Democratic Party wants them to believe. Obamacare was only a stepping-stone toward a single payer healthcare system (as advocated by socialist Senator Bernie Sanders) where everyone is totally dependent on government for healthcare.

That's not what the Founders wanted when they declared independence and wrote a constitution for limited government. They wanted people to be independent of government to the greatest extent possible. That is called freedom. Only free people can truly realize their full potential. Independent people feel capable and confident. Dependent people feel vulnerable and afraid.

Shouldn't our elected representatives be trying to develop a healthcare system that makes us feel confident that we are capable of managing our own health? Of course, in any large population there will be some, because of various reasons, that are not capable of managing their own health and that need the assistance of government or a charitable organization. And healthcare may be too costly for the very poor. But the majority of free people in a free country should be able to afford and manage their own healthcare. The question is how to do this?

The free market economic system works for healthcare just like other sectors of the economy but for the free market system to work prices must be meaningful to consumers. Everything the government under Republican and Democratic administrations has done for decades has been to reduce the impact of prices on healthcare consumers. As a result, the cost of healthcare has skyrocketed. Healthcare now absorbs 17% of the economy, far more than any other country on Earth. Not only can people not afford to pay for healthcare, the country can't afford to pay for healthcare at these prices.

The cost of Lasik surgery, which is not covered by most insurance policies (which are not really insurance), has plummeted. The cost of Lasik surgery in 1998 was $2200 per eye but you can get it now for $250 per eye (a reduction of 89%). But the cost of "insured" procedures has gone the opposite direction. Do you know how much your doctor charges your insurance company for an office visit or a procedure? Do you care? No! You don't care! The price is irrelevant to you and as long as prices are irrelevant costs will keep going up.

Wait a minute, our progressive friends will say. Government will control prices and that will control the spiraling costs. The Soviets tried that. It didn't work (see, Whatever Happened to the Invisible Hand of Capitalism? by Vitaliy Katsenelson who grew up in the Soviet Union). Progressives won't be happy until the government has its hand in everything we do – not just healthcare. What happens to our freedom and independence then?

No single healthcare bill can fix our healthcare system once and for all. Our legislators need to develop a process that can unwind decades of well intentioned but wrong-headed policies that are too numerous to mention in a brief article. It will take time for competition to wring out the high prices and to make sure that health insurance is not applied routine costs but extraordinary expenses (like other kinds of insurance). But it is about time that our elected representatives start working to preserve and increase our freedom and stop creating new entitlements that will slowly (but surely) enslave us.

2018 Perspective.

2017: A Trumpian Year in Review

A Bold Idea (about Taxes)
June 26, 2017
Victor C. Bolles

When I first heard the idea of eliminating net interest expense deductions in the proposed GOP tax reform plan, I thought it was a terrible idea. But the more I think about it the more I like it, especially when it is combined with another GOP tax reform – the immediate deduction of capital investment.

Currently, if you borrow money to invest in a capital asset, you get to deduct the interest expense on the loan but you have spread the cost of the capital asset over many years through an annual depreciation of the original expense. If the asset depreciates over ten years then it will take ten years for you to fully deduct the cost of the investment. The government is front loading their collections of taxes and you have to wait to get the tax benefit of your investment. The current tax law also allows you to deduct your interest expense on any money you borrowed to make the investment but you are not able to deduct the expense of any dividends you pay to your equity investors (unless your company is an S corporation or a partnership). In my book, *Principled Policy* (2016), I had argued to make dividends tax deductible but the GOP proposal takes it the other way.

The current tax treatment punishes equity investment with higher costs and rewards borrowing with lower costs. This has resulted in higher amounts of leverage in our corporations. Higher leverage increases financial risk making them more vulnerable to business downturns and bankruptcies.

The non-deductibility of net interest expense will increase the cost of doing business but not as much as I had originally thought. Unless you are in a very highly leveraged company or in a very low margin business, the elimination of net interest expense deduction will have only a small impact on your earnings. If you are so highly leveraged that the lack of interest deductibility severely impacts your earnings then you are investing in assets with low margins that cannot support so much debt. Implementing this tax reform will discourage excess leverage and make the country less susceptible to recessions.

By allowing the immediate deduction of capital investments, the government is back loading the collection of taxes and giving you the upfront benefit of your investment. Depending on the type of industry a company is in, a large capital investment could substantially reduce taxes owed (which is why the government prefers extended depreciation). Fast growing companies might not pay any taxes at all for many years. Democrats and progressives might think this is horrible but, if you think about it, more investment contributes to GDP and employment so this reform would accelerate growth and provide jobs (increasing taxes by increasing taxpayers and reducing the need for welfare expenditures).

Coming from the financial industry, I was concerned about how these reforms would impact banks and other financial companies. But financial companies usually have net interest income instead of a net interest loss. Net interest income is used to pay for most of all the other expenses of running a financial company. Financial companies usually fail because of asset/liability mismanagement, excessive leverage or illiquidity (usually in combination) and not so much due to losses from negative spreads. If a financial company had a negative interest spread it would likely have no income and therefor would pay no income tax anyway. The lack of interest deductibility would only affect their tax loss carry forward if and when they return to profitability.

The elimination of net interest expense deduction would also square corporate taxation with the taxation of individuals (except in the case of the mortgage interest deduction which I have also advocated to be eliminated). Technically, for philosophical precision, individuals should be able offset their interest income with their income expenses but, since most individuals except the very rich have much more interest expense than income I doubt our tax hawks in DC would allow that.

So the elimination of net interest expense as a deduction and allowing immediate deduction of capital investments from corporate taxes would increase the cost of debt, reduce the incentive to increase leverage, promote investment and reduce the chance of recession. I think that's a good thing. The major risk to this reform, and it is indeed a major reform, will be efforts by industry associations and special interests to carve out exceptions and special treatment to this overall policy shift. Congress would then be pushed to reduce the effectiveness of this reform by allowing all sorts of special treatment to specific individuals and companies. This is precisely the problem with the current tax system and why it is so badly in need of reform. It would be a shame if a bold idea such as this would be reduced to a 5,000-page modification to the tax code that only impacts those that lack clout in Washington.

2018 Perspective: The Tax Cut and Jobs Act of 2017 did not fully implement the proposed elimination of the deduction for net interest expense allowing the deduction of up to 30 percent of earnings. While not as clean as the original proposal it should have some beneficial impact on the economy. However, the 30 percent allowance will motivate corporations and their advisors to seek ways to avoid this limitation.

July 2017

Not Too Much to Ask For

July 5, 2017
Victor C. Bolles

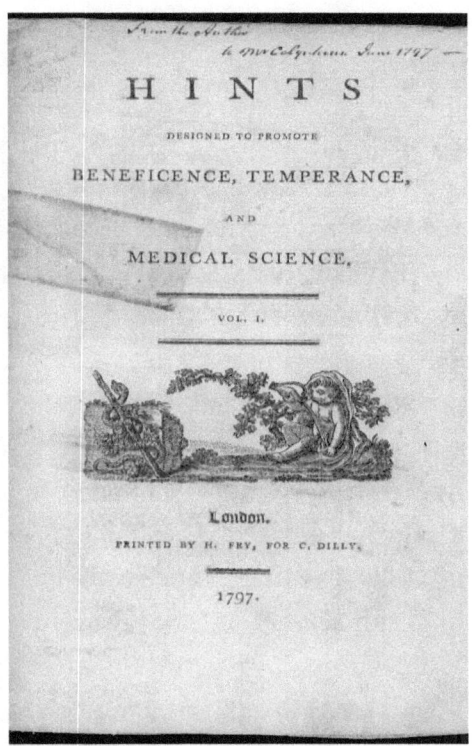

Welcome Images

Okay. This essay may be a bit repetitive to some of my faithful readers but perhaps if you think it is of value you can share this with your friends or (better) your elected representatives.

So voting on the Senate version of the GOP healthcare has been postponed until after the Fourth of July recess. The senators apparently cannot figure out how to manipulate the delivery of healthcare entitlements to our entitlement-addicted populace without it costing an arm and a leg (or more importantly the next election).

Trumpcare will not be "great" or "beautiful" any more than Obamacare. All the swapping around of benefits and costs is just so much moving of deck chairs on the Titanic. They do not address the rising costs or the underlying problems of the American healthcare system. One has to wonder why healthcare is so expensive while every other product or service provided via our free market economic system (from our daily bread to flat panel TVs) is so cheap.

Motivated by good intentions, the American healthcare system has been going off track for almost a century. Innocently enough, it began as a benefit that companies offered to attract qualified employees during World War II when many men were in the military and qualified applicants were in short supply. Employees liked this benefit and companies kept them after the war was over. Insurance companies liked the benefit because employed people were a good demographic for their insurance plans (generally healthy with healthy families and money to pay for uncovered procedures). Most insurance was for catastrophic illness and did not pay for office visits or well-baby visits (it was – after all – insurance). Even some of the covered procedures required the insured person to pay for a portion of the cost so the healthcare consumer was not totally immune to healthcare costs.

Congress thought that this was a great thing so they tried to make it even easier for companies to provide this benefit by making the cost of the benefit tax deductible for the company but not taxable to the beneficiary. This was great except that over time more and more procedures became covered by insurance in order to take advantage of the tax break. So slowly the healthcare consumer became more and more immunized against healthcare costs while, at the same time, healthcare coverage was transformed from a benefit to a taxpayer-subsidized right.

Also, because consumers are immune to the cost, the cost of healthcare has increased much faster the any other service in the economy. Healthcare now consumes 17% of the US economy - far more than any other country but providing only mediocre results. The excess we spend (nearly a trillion dollars annually) is simply wasted.

Healthcare is not production. It is maintenance. If a factory operator spent almost a fifth of his expenses on maintenance he would be fired. You need to spend enough on maintenance to keep the factory running but spending more is wasted and eats into profits or some other necessary expense. Right now America (in essence) must skimp on maintaining our infrastructure (and other necessary expenses) to maintain our human capital. The cost structure is all bolloxed up.

So what is a country going to do? Senator Elizabeth Warren wants to create a single payer healthcare system along the lines of Europe and some other developed countries (we already have a single payer system operating in the US. It's called the Veterans Administration). A single payer system sounds like a simple fix. Just have the government do it. If it's so easy why not have the government run everything? Senator Warren and Senator Bernie Sanders would be happy with that. While you're at it, let's include a universal basic income (UBI) for everybody in the country. Then we would have a population that was medicated, protected and coddled to the satisfaction of the progressives.

But such people would be Americans in name only. They bear no resemblance to our ancestors that made America great. Our ancestors were risk takers independent of government not dependent on government and afraid to take any responsibility for their own lives.

It was the free market economic system that made America the most powerful economy in the world. There is nothing essentially different about healthcare than any other sector of the economy except the left has beaten it into us that healthcare is a right and that we should brook no opposition to free universal healthcare.

What we currently have is a cost plus contract. According to Wikipedia "A cost-plus contract, also termed a cost reimbursement contract, is a contract where a contractor is paid for all of its allowed expenses, plus additional payment to allow for a profit." Many government contracts are cost plus such as the Big Dig tunnel in Boston. Originally budgeted for $2.8 billion it is now expected to end up costing $22 billion because the contractor low-balled the bid and then said "oh. We have these extra expenses. You need to cover them in the contract or we will have to stop work." So what do you do? You have three choices, 1) stop the work and have a big unusable hole in the ground and billions already spent, 2) hire a new contractor who will have to start from scratch and will encounter the same "extra" expenses as the first contractor or 3) add the "extra" expenses to the contract.

Healthcare is a lot like that. If you get a bill from a surgery you will see that you are charged for every cotton swab and sponge used in the operation, plus every physician's assistant that poked his or her head into the operating room. Ask your doctor how much a procedure will cost and he will likely tell you that he has no idea. The price is meaningless because it has no impact. It is handled by the back-office and sent to the insurance company or Medicare to take care of.

The only way to get a great American healthcare system is to let the free market system work its magic. But free market does not mean laissez faire. The government still has an important role to play, that of regulator – something it cannot do as operator. There are some problems that need to be solved such as portability, pre-existing conditions and so forth. And there will still be some government assistance; some people will be too poor to pay for even affordable healthcare (solving poverty being one of the other areas where massive government involvement has not been effective).

Australia has been able to construct a relatively efficient healthcare system where consumers pay a portion of the cost so they are aware of prices and shop for healthcare as assiduously as a fashionista at TJMaxx. They still complain about the cost which at 9% of GDP is about half that of the US. If the free market economic system helped America's rise to prominence why are we so willing to abandon it in such an important part of our lives?

Any healthcare bill passed by Congress that actually addresses these fundamental problems will not be great or beautiful immediately. True reform will take many years to implement. Too many people are locked into the current system and cannot extricate themselves from being dependent on it. It will take a generation to undo the distortions created by government's good intentions but it is not too much to ask for both affordable healthcare and our freedom and independence.

2018 Perspective. As you know, nothing was done so we are still in the same mess we were in before.

In Praise of Self-Interest

July 14, 2017
Victor C. Bolles

Why does self-interest get such a bad rap? Isn't everyone one who has a strong self-interest a greedy, self-centered narcissist (like you know who)? Wouldn't the world be a better place if we were all altruists? But the struggle of mankind to suppress self-interest and promote altruism has gotten us in as much trouble as self-interest.

Let me explain. As Darwin noted, all organisms aspire to self-preservation and procreation. Self-preservation prolongs the period for procreation and improves the chances that the organism will be able to pass on its DNA to future generations. Animals do not have a whiff of altruism in their bones and have scant inclination to assist other members of their species except their own offspring (which contain their DNA – see above).

Self-interest is an offshoot of the instinct of self-preservation. To have self-interest you must be aware of your self (which most other organisms are not). Once you are aware of yourself you do things to better yourself. You try to eat the best food, find the best spot in the cave or get the best animal pelt to keep you warm during the frigid nights of the last ice age. If someone else has better food or a better pelt it would be in your best interest to take it from him (or her). Of course it might not be in your best interest if the other person picked up a rock and smacked you in the head for taking their stuff.

Life during the ice age was nasty, brutish and short (to borrow a phrase). To remedy this dire circumstance Thomas Hobbes recommended that a powerful authority (indeed a leviathan) should rule in order to make people cooperate and to suppress predatory self-interest. It was not long after the end of the ice age and the rise of agriculture that human civilization invented kings and religions to suppress and control the self-interest of the people (but not the self-interest of the king or the priests).

In the Nineteenth Century Karl Marx (and others) witnessed the depredations of the Industrial Revolution and felt that the self-interested actions of capitalists led to the exploitation of the workers. He felt that only the state should own capital and that workers should live by the saying "from each according to his ability, to each according to his need." Of course, most people are not sufficiently altruistic to abide by Marx's admonition so a communist society requires a dictatorship of the proletariat the suppress the self-interests of such newly liberated laborers until such time as they are so ethically advanced as to become "Communist Man (sorry, girls. Marx was not much of a feminist)".

Of course Hobbes' monarchical leviathans were doomed as Parliaments asserted their authority to limit the monarch's ability to act in his (or her) own self-interest. The rule of law (as conceived by Enlightenment philosophers) meant that the self-interest of no man (or woman) was above the law. The social contract was thought to provide the framework for our dealing with our fellow man (or woman) and a democratic government of, by and for the people was created to assure that individuals in the society acted in accordance to the social contract.

Adam Smith famously stated "It is not from the benevolence of the butcher, the brewer, or the baker that we expect our dinner, but from their regard to their own interest". This is the magic of the free market economic system. Within the framework of the social contract people can act in their own self-interest while benefitting their fellow citizens at the same time.

Of course, as we look back across history from our perch here in the twenty-first century we see that this wonderful free market system has not performed up to its specs. The framework of the social contract has been distorted to work in favor of the self-interest of certain powerful parties and against the self-interest of other (less powerful) parties. This has occurred because our officials elected to represent our interest have themselves self-interests that have been manipulated for the powerful parties we spoke of earlier.

Our altruistic friends of the progressive persuasion are outraged at this turn of events (among other things). Their answer is to suppress self-interest (which they have labeled "greed" and "profits") by taxing the wealthy who have presumably become so wealthy in order to satisfy their greed (i.e.; self-interest) through the exploitation of others (see Marx, above). Further, they want to control parts of the economy deemed most cruel and exploitive (such as healthcare) through government domination. Don't worry; salvation of housing and food distribution is coming.

It was Founder John Adams who said, "Remember, democracy never lasts long. It soon wastes, exhausts, and murders itself. There never was a democracy yet that did not commit suicide." Well, I think we lasted longer than President Adams thought we would but our progressive friends are working hard to make his prediction come true. But the progressives' bold plans are dependent on the altruism of government bureaucrats and elected officials (whose self-interests permitted the distortion of the social contract in the first place). Unfortunately, the advent of the Communist Man who works for the benefit of others and not for himself (or herself) has not yet come about.

The answer to our dilemma is not to suppress our natural desire to work in our own self-interest, but to put self-interest to work as described by Adam Smith. If a greedy person provides me with a good product or service at a competitive price what do I care about his motives? It is only when greed distorts the social contract by providing shoddy goods or charging monopolistic prices that we must become concerned. The enforcement of the framework of the social contract by government is supposed to prevent such actions. If the social contract has been captured by special interests then we must work to restore the contract so that it can function as designed.

Self-interest is not the villain here. Self-interest is a powerful motivating source and civilization needs powerful motivating sources in order to function. Any powerful force can be used for good or ill (think: fire, electricity, atomic power). It is up to us to channel this source of power for the good of our free and democratic society.

2018 Perspective. Unbounded energy has no power. The energy latent in gasoline must be contained in a cylinder in order to power an automobile. In the same manner, the energy latent in self-interest must be bounded by the social contract to power our economy and society.

Righteous Thinking and Foolish Nature

July 17, 2017
Victor C. Bolles

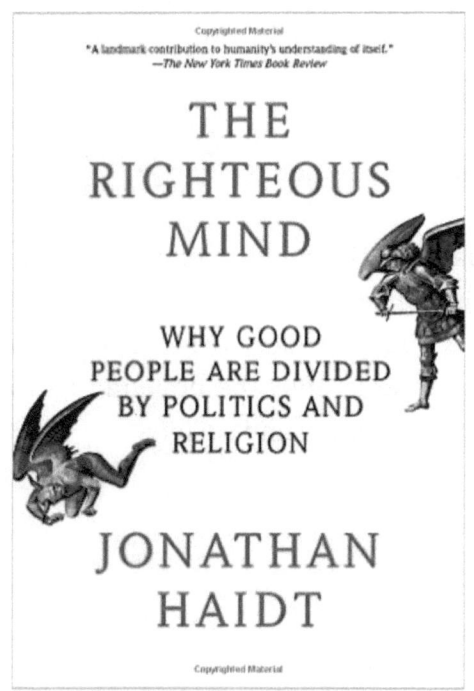

Daniel Kahneman, a psychologist, won the Nobel Prize for Economics (actually the Swedish National Bank's Prize in Economic Sciences in memory of Alfred Nobel) for his academic work in establishing behavioral economics. In his popular book, *Thinking Fast and Slow (2013)*, he explained that the human brain has two systems. System one thinks fast and system two thinks slow. I call system one the intuitive brain and system two the rational brain. Much of economic theory is based on the assumption that people usually employ their rational brain to make economic decisions. Professor Kahneman showed that this is often not the case. In fact many people use their intuitive brain almost exclusively and almost all of us use our intuitive brain very often (which is why economists can rarely predict economic events with any accuracy).

Jonathan Haidt is also a psychologist and a professor at New York University but dedicates his scientific experiments into the psychology of politics. He has a similar understanding of the human brain and how it operates as Professor Kahneman. The key difference between them is that, while Kahneman believes that the rational brain is lazy and only takes charge in difficult cases where higher level thinking is required, Haidt believes that the intuitive brain is almost always in charge and the rational brain's primary function is to think up rational reasons for doing what the intuitive brain already decided on doing. This makes us less rational beings than even Kahneman posited and in the current American political environment that is not a good thing.

The current level of political thinking in America is basically that if I am a good person and I believe that public policy should go in a certain direction then anyone who opposes my position must (by definition) be a bad person and their policy preferences evil. This type of thinking has not only led to the current political impasse confronting us but has fostered the low level of political discourse that leads to hate and, potentially, violence. Haidt set out to discover the basis for this problem and what he (an admitted liberal and lifelong Democrat) discovered surprised him.

Haidt has used Moral Foundations Theory as the basis for his analysis. Moral Foundations Theory defines five moral axes as the basis for a system of moral belief; care/harm, fairness/cheating, loyalty/betrayal, authority/subversion, and sanctity/degradation. Haidt later added the axis of liberty/oppression, which is particularly relevant in political discussions.

What Haidt found in a series of surveys with liberals (better described as progressives), conservatives and libertarians (or classical liberals) was that liberals rated caring and fairness as the most important moral foundations while conservatives rated all the elements as more or less equally important. Haidt found that liberals not only placed less importance on elements such as loyalty, authority and sanctity but that found that they are essentially blind to these moral precepts and cannot credit actions based on those precepts. They condemn conservative principles as evil because they cannot see the moral justification for their actions.

Further, Haidt found that libertarians had a moral structure more similar to liberals than conservatives but with some differences. Libertarians placed much greater emphasis on liberty than did liberals (makes sense). He also found that, while libertarians gave great importance to fairness, their concept of fairness (if you have read any of my other essays or books you know what I think of fairness as the basis for policy) is very different. Liberals view fairness as equality while libertarians view fairness as proportionality. So while liberals would say that equal access to healthcare is fair, libertarians would say that somebody that worked harder should get paid more. You can easily see how these two concepts of fairness would be at loggerheads in the development of tax policy.

Does this mean we are doomed to continue flying past each other on our different moral compasses, unable to agree on anything? I don't think so. Professor Haidt's analysis indicates that the actions of most people have a moral basis and that people of other political persuasions are not evil. Conservatives don't want poor people to die any more than liberals want to destroy western civilization.

If Professor Haidt is correct in his hypothesis that our moral sense originates in our intuitive brain (and that our rational brain primarily develops reasons to support our gut feelings), then rational arguments will do little to sway people from their heartfelt beliefs. Outraged fury on the left and right with the potential to descend into violence will only harden these feelings. Reasoning will not change the others' position on any issue. So how do we escape from this impasse? Compromise!

If you think about it, the differences between the left and right are complementary. The left represents new thinking, change and renewal. Societies need change and renewal or they will ossify and begin to decay. The right tries to hold on to long-held traditions and values. Too much change too quickly can tear societies apart and descend into anarchy or civil war. A democratic society that goes back and forth between left and right can incorporate necessary change while providing time for cherished traditions to adapt top modern innovations. Any democratic society without both a left and right will be doomed to one extreme or the other.

Professor Haidt's concept of two types of fairness gives us insight on how to approach the country's problems that we share in common. As conceived by the founders, America is supposed to be a meritocracy, which would imply proportional fairness over absolute equality. But proportional fairness does not imply that people should starve or be without healthcare. Strict proportional fairness is as unfair as an absolute equality of fairness. (Which is why I recommend a standard of "not too unfair" in the development of public policy in *Principled Policy (2016)*). If we can agree on policies that the opposing groups can all agree are "not too unfair" then we have created the possibility of compromise. No side will get their perfectly ideal policy. But maybe we can get a policy that actually works.

I would recommend that everyone read Professor Haidt's book, the *Righteous Mind (2013)*. You do not have to agree with every aspect of his hypotheses to gain insight to our human nature and the basis for our moral systems. Political ideology must sometimes defer to scientific investigation. Between Kahneman, Haidt and others we are gaining insight into our human nature and we would be foolish to ignore these discoveries.

But, of course, we are foolish, aren't we?

2018 Perspective. If anything we have become even more foolish in 2018 than in 2017. The opposing camps of left and right are farther apart than ever and more extreme in their positions. Perhaps only the inevitable crisis would produce a leader who can reconcile the opposing parties into what we all aspire to be – Americans.

ZombieCare

July 25, 2017
Victor C. Bolles

The GOP healthcare bill just won't die and go away. It keeps coming back in an ever more grotesque form. It is actually more like Frankenstein's monster (if I can mix my monster metaphor), made up of bits and pieces scavenged from some graveyard in order to appease this or that Republican. Now that I think about it, the healthcare bill is more like a zombie Frankenstein's monster. That's really scary.

I am getting really tired of writing about healthcare because there are so many other things that need to get done. Like a zombie's relentless search for human flesh, Republicans keep trying to come up with ways to keep the healthcare entitlement without calling it an entitlement. Whether you pay for it with a subsidy or a tax benefit, it's still an entitlement. No one (except maybe Rand Paul) is giving a thought about why you need an entitlement for healthcare. It's the high cost, dummies. Even wealthy people can go broke trying to pay for healthcare. But even government can go broke paying for healthcare, which is why we need to solve this problem.

Neither Obamacare nor the proposed GOP replacement solves the problem of the ever-increasing cost of healthcare that currently gobbles up 17% of our economy and wastes a trillion dollars a year. They are both chicken wire and chewing gum amalgams intended to provide an entitlement while meeting the needs of special interest groups while at the same time appealing to the extreme bases that each party is beholden to. If that sounds like an impossible task, you are right. It is impossible.

What the two opposing sides don't want to do is to address the real problem. There are essentially two ways to get medical costs back down from the stratosphere. One is a single payer system favored by progressives and socialists. The other is a free market system favored libertarians and right-wingers where competition drives down prices while improving the product or service.

Most other developed economies have already converted to a single payer system. But to me, going to a single payer system is like giving up. It is like saying that we humans are incapable of managing our own affairs and that we need big brother or a nanny to take care of us. I think too highly of human beings to think that we must put ourselves at the mercy of a higher power for our most basic necessities. And, of course, that higher power is not God or some omniscient being, but other humans to whom we willingly sacrifice our freedom in return for their supposed beneficence.

As Winston Churchill said, "you can count on Americans to do the right thing – after they've tried everything else." Obamacare and the GOP's attempts to create TrumpCare should tell us that we have just about exhausted all the other possible ways of solving this dilemma.

In order to fix healthcare in the US, we need to deconstruct the current zombie-like monstrosity instead of adding something new to it (making it even more monstrous). This will not be an easy task (which is why most politicians are not proposing anything like this). Easy or not, we must either create a market-oriented healthcare system that is efficient and affordable or we will be relegated to a VA-like single payer system that can control costs through government fiat. Tell me, which one seems more like the American way to you?

2018 Perspective. The only good news is that the Republicans have given up on healthcare reform. Meanwhile

2017: A Trumpian Year in Review

Democrats are basing their 2018 election campaign on instituting a single payer system. Oh, brother!

August 2017

RAISE-ing a Ruckus

August 4, 2017
Victor C. Bolles

From the plaque on the Statue of Liberty, The New Colossus, by Emma Lazarus (1883)

At a raucous press briefing presidential adviser Stephen Miller announced the White House's proposal to update America's legal immigration process. The Reforming American Immigration for a Strong Economy (RAISE) Act will be sponsored in Congress by Senators Tom Cotton and David Perdue. The RAISE Act will strictly limit the immigration of unskilled workers, reduce the ability of legal US residents to bring in their extended family and eliminate the Diversity Visa lottery. The RAISE Act only deals with immigrants coming to the United States as legal residents (green card holders) and does not deal with the issue of undocumented (illegal) immigrants.

America is a land of immigrants. My ancestors immigrated to North America. Yours did, too. Even Native Americans' ancestors immigrated here across an ice age generated land bridge (or other method yet unknown). Many came to flee from religious oppression in Europe. Others came fleeing famine or war. Some came in first class cabins and some came in steerage.

But America was not always welcoming to immigrants. The Naturalization Act of 1790 limited citizenship to free white persons of good character. The Chinese Exclusion Act of 1882 blocked the immigration of Chinese and other Asians. The Emergency Quota Act (1921) and the Immigration Act of 1924 limited the number immigrants by national origin to 3% of the number of such residents in the 1910 census (i.e.; before the waves of immigrants from Eastern and Southern Europe). The Immigration and Nationality Act of 1965 eliminated the quotas based on the National Origins Formula and created a new formula that maintained country limits but provided exceptions based on family relationships and skills. Conservative Democrats had insisted on including family relationships because they thought it would promote a continuance of the then current racial structure of the country. But the family relationships exception led to chain migration where one family member opens the door to a host of relatives. Chain migration totally frustrated the intent of the country limits and has led to the much more ethnically diverse United States that we now live in.

So the welcoming Lady Liberty of Emma Lazarus' sonnet was not actually so welcoming and laws aimed at maintaining the racial and ethnic structure of the country have had the opposite effect. Rapidly changing demographics can be disruptive to a society leading to a backlash by those that feel that they have been displaced. While we shouldn't go back the old racist quota system, we should avoid having an immigration policy purposefully disruptive to our society.

The RAISE Act will cut back on the types of family relationships that qualify for the exceptions to visa limits and include a skills-based merit system that will cut back on lower-skilled immigrants. Critics claim this is nothing more than disguised racism designed to appease President Trump's base of "deplorables". They scoffed at Miller's assertion that they wanted to limit lower-skilled workers in order to preserve employment opportunities for US ethnic minorities. In the press conference there was a heated battle of studies on the impact of foreign-born workers on low wage jobs. Various studies have come to opposing opinions on the impact of the immigration of low skilled workers but whatever the impact it can't be that great or the outcomes of the studies would be clearer.

Nevertheless, a Bureau of Labor Statistics study shows that the unemployment rate of foreign-born ethnic minorities is lower than for natives so there may be something to Miller's contention (white foreign-born workers on the other hand had a higher unemployment rate than natives).

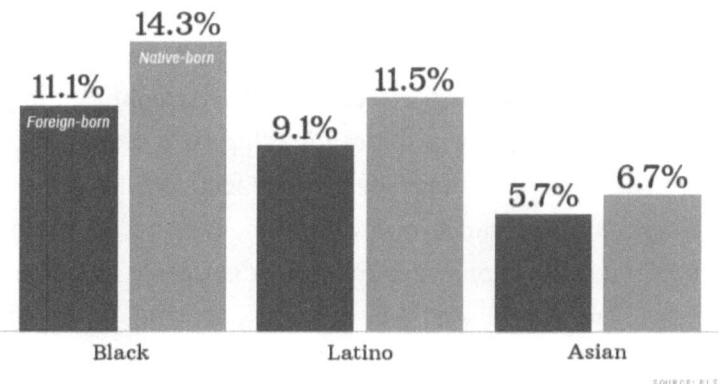

It was Mr. Miller's contention in the press conference that the RAISE Act was a very focused policy that only affected green card holders and was not intended to resolve other immigration issues such as undocumented aliens and Deferred Action on Childhood Arrivals (DACA). But if the goal of the RAISE Act is to strengthen the US economy the Trump Administration needs to address the issue of temporary workers in this bill or in a parallel bill.

Two vital sectors of the US economy are having severe problems finding workers and the impact is slowing down US economic growth. The Los Angeles Times reports that farmers are paying up to $16/hour for agricultural workers and that this cost is being reflected in higher food prices and shortages. While $16/hour is not a bad wage, it may not be very good for a seasonal worker living in the US trying to stretch his harvest bonus through a long winter. But if he were spending the winter back in Mexico or Central America his earnings would go a lot further.

Likewise, US new home sales are falling because construction companies cannot find enough workers to build the houses. The Bracero program after WWII was relatively successful until the unions shut it down, A well-designed temporary worker program that assures that the incoming workers are well treated and fairly paid should be able to relieve this bottleneck and allow the US economy to expand.

Another provision of the proposed bill would limit refugees to 50,000 a year. Any limit on refugees, however, should allow the President the flexibility to respond to future crises the size of which we cannot predict (such as the influx of Vietnamese refugees after the end of the Viet Nam War).

Finally, the RAISE Act would eliminate the diversity lottery program that randomly selects 55,000 people around the world to come to the US in the name of diversity (they do have to pass some background checks). Diversity for diversity's sake is senseless and under the current system these new arrivals would then be allowed to bring in a slew of their relatives as well, which would greatly increase the impact of such a program (for a more complete discussion of diversity, please see my June 16, 2016 post, *On Diversity*). Rather than randomly selecting people for some vague notion such as diversity, the visas reserved for the lottery could be added to the merit based visa program. The old limits were set when the United States had a smaller population and are out of date. The US is less welcoming on a per capita basis than other countries using a merit based system such as Canada and Australia.

So with some minor changes, the RAISE Act would be a step forward in developing a reasoned and principled immigration policy (of course the hardest part is yet to come). Now it is up to the inept Republican controlled Congress to pass this proposal. You might think it difficult to get bipartisan support for any Trump proposal. But in reality, President Trump should not take credit for this bill (nor should Mr. Miller). It is an almost exact copy of the 1995 recommendation of the Commission on Immigration Reform commissioned by President Bill Clinton and chaired by noted liberal, Barbara Jordan. The only thing really bad about this bill is that President Trump chose the annoying Mr. Miller to present it.

2018 Perspective. The RAISE Act went nowhere in Congress and US immigration policy is an even bigger mess than it was in 2017. The devil is in the details and the details of the RAISE Act proved to be so onerous that it could find little support. President Trump tried to rescind DACA and force Congress to move forward on both DACA and the RAISE Act. DACA has been tied up in the courts so nothing has been

.

Bias vs. Bias

August 9, 2017
Victor C. Bolles

On Monday morning (August 7, 2017), Google CEO Sundar Pichai fired an employee, James Damore, for writing a memo stating that Google's diversity program was based on left wing ideology and not on the biological and/or psychological reasons that explain why the proportion of women in tech jobs and leadership roles is less than that of men. Mr. Pichai stated that while many of the points raised should be discussed, the core assertion of the memo, that men and women are different and that these differences favor men in a company such as Google, was crass gender stereotyping and violated the company's code of conduct.

But Mr. Damore does not appear to be a misogynistic troglodyte. He cites numerous articles from well-respected publications (US New and World Report and the Atlantic Monthly, for example) and several peer-reviewed psychological studies to support his assertions. He cites several scientists and authors that readers of my essays will be familiar with including Jonathan Haidt (*The Righteous Mind*, 2012) and Scott E. Paige, (*The Difference*, 2008).

Mr. Damore asserted that in a company with a corporate culture that rewards hard work, long hours and assertive behavior, men are more likely to thrive than women. He stated that women are more collaborative than men and relate more to relationships than to things as do men. Mr. Damore suggested that the company's gender equality goals would be better served by less bashing men with diversity training and more by structuring the work environment to reward collaboration.

He stated that women suffer from a higher degree of neuroticism (backed by a peer-reviewed study) that does not function very well in a high-stress job place such as Google. This comment generated a lot of outrage among women in tech including Sheryl Sandburg who averred that unequal outcomes in tech are not related to gender differences but to cultural stereotypes.

But Mr. Damore titled his memo "Google's Ideological Echo Chamber". His concern is that there is more ideological discrimination than gender discrimination at Google. Perhaps this assertion prompted his firing more than accusing women of neuroticism as it hits a bit closer to the locus of Google's problem. One of the great problems confronting our country is the divisive nature of American politics where partisans on both sides of the political aisle are locked in feedback loops of alt-left and alt-right propaganda outlets that spew reams of fake news. This is Mr. Damore's point when he says that discrimination to reach an ideologically based outcome is "unfair, divisive and bad for business".

Professor Paige, in his book, showed that diverse people working toward a common goal generated better results than less diverse groups. But Professor Paige was talking about diversity in ways of thinking. In solving a difficult technical problem a mathematician and physicist would complement each other even if of the same sex. Two mathematicians might not be complementary even if of different sexes.

Professor Haidt while addressing the annual meeting of the Society for Personality and Social Psychology asked the group of about a thousand participants for a show of hands, how many are liberal? About eighty percent of the hands went up. Next were centrists and moderates. By the time it came down to libertarians it was twelve hands up and for conservatives, three. The point is not that academia is liberal. We know that. It is that the choices of their studies and the way they structure their questionnaires is within this left-wing framework and the results reflect this bias. This is called confirmation bias and it is common in people and non-diverse groups. That is where you need diversity. And this was the point Mr. Damore was making and why he was fired.

Postscript: A study that was reported in Fortune Magazine, said that woman CEOs of public companies had almost three times the ROI (Return on Investment) of male CEOs. The study by Catalyst (a women's issue NGO) showed that a group of 80 women CEOs outperformed the S&P (as a proxy for male CEOs) by 226% over a twelve-year period from 2002 until 2014. The study is not definitive and it did not correct for women CEOs in the S&P or the size/industry of the companies but it does give an indication that women make pretty darn good CEOs. Today's guest host on Squawk Box (Kevin O'Leary from Shark Tank) prefers to invest with woman run companies. But a woman would have a difficult time rising to CEO in a highly competitive and aggressive corporate culture such as Google. Perhaps Mr. Pichai would be better off working with Mr. Damore to change Google corporate culture than firing him. And hire a couple of conservatives to reduce confirmation bias if he can find some in Silicon Valley.

2018 Perspective. James Damore and other complainants are suing Google. This may take a while.

Robt E. Lee

August 15, 2017
Victor C. Bolles

On Saturday, August 12th a "Unite the Right" rally in Charlottesville, VA to protest the removal of a statue of General Robert E. Lee descended into chaos and violence. The protestors were an amalgam of extreme right-wing nuts including skinheads, Neo-Nazis and Ku Klux Klanners so the violence was preordained. They were met by counter-protesters equally prepared for combat. So there was combat and one death when one of Neo-Nazi nuts decided to use his car as a lethal weapon.

It is sad that all this hate and violence was about a statue of General Lee who I have always considered to be a good man in a bad position. Lee came from a prominent Virginia family that had fallen on hard times. He graduated from West Point and was an officer in the US Army for 32 years. He was a founder of St. Marks Episcopal Church in San Antonio where my family and I went to church for many years. He was an engineer and mapmaker just like my great granddaddy and they were both officers in the Confederate Army. He also gave a speech from my great granddaddy's porch in 1869. So I have always had an affinity for the General but he chose unwisely when he resigned his commission and joined the South. My great granddaddy made the same unwise choice but back then the country was still young and many people's loyalty was to their state and not the nation.

It is hard for us here in the twenty-first century to think in nineteenth century terms. Slavery had been common throughout recorded history. The Bible and the Quran accept the condition of slavery although they both provide guidelines on the proper treatment of slaves. Ancient agriculture was vey labor intensive such that large numbers of slaves were economically necessary. But in the nineteenth century things were beginning to change.

Many people, including some slaveholders, came to see this practice as morally repugnant. Slavery is not compatible with Western Enlightenment philosophy as expressed in the Declaration of Independence. All men (and women) are created equal. Equal in rights and they should be equal in opportunity. There was a growing movement of people and groups opposed to the institution of slavery in the United States, especially in the North.

In addition, the economic progress brought on by the Industrial Revolution reduced the economic incentive of slavery. In 1800 83% of the US population was engaged in agriculture. By the eve of the Civil War in 1860 this percentage was down to 53%. Now it is 2%. Thanks to mechanization, slavery would soon make less and less sense. The only slavery that still exists in the Western world is the sex trafficking of people because of the illegal profits it generates.

George Washington and Thomas Jefferson were both slaveholders and, while they knew that this practice must be eliminated, they both had difficulty extricating themselves from owning slaves. George Washington freed his slaves on his death but not those owned by his wife, Martha. Jefferson proposed several plans to eliminate slavery in the new nation but nothing came to fruition.

People live out their lives in confusion about the events swirling around them, a fog that only becomes clear with the passage of time. Just as we lack perspective on the events going around us, so our ancestors also suffered from a lack of perspective. What we now see as clear pathways they saw as blind alleys and dead-ends.

But just because it is difficult to put ourselves in the shoes of nineteenth century plantation owners and understand the quandary that slavery presented to them does not mean we should glorify this past. Our current age is built on the discoveries and mistakes of past eras. But they are eras in and of the past and we, with our hard won knowledge, cannot afford to go back in time to a more primitive era. The antebellum South may have been a paradise for wealthy planters but it was hell on earth for many others. It is time to take the Confederate statues down. Put them in museums so that we do not forget our past but do not present them as symbols of something admirable. Their only redeeming value is not for the past they represent but for insight into the mindset of the people that put these statues on display and those that seek to keep them on display. I respect my southern heritage but I am glad the North won the Civil War.

2018 Perspective. Removal of the statues of Confederate generals and memorials to the Confederacy continue to take place. School districts in the South are changing the names of schools to eliminate the glorification of the Confederacy and its peculiar institution (slavery).

What is Winning?
August 24, 2017
Victor C. Bolles

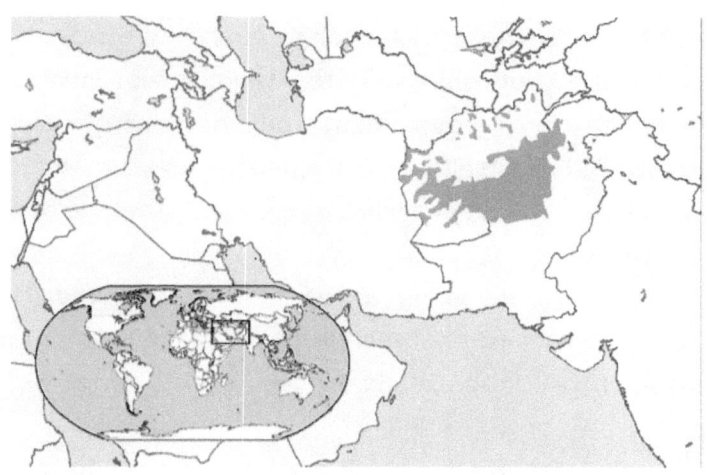

In a nationally broadcast speech, President Trump announced a new policy for the fighting in Afghanistan. The main elements of the new policy (troop levels and our policy toward Pakistan) reflect the thinking of the Armed Forces chiefs. But the focus of the policy is to win the war in Afghanistan.

President Trump stated, "we send our bravest to defeat our enemies overseas -- and we will always win." And further, "But one way or another, these problems will be solved. I'm a problem solver. And in the end, we will win." And finally, "Our troops will fight to win. We will fight to win."

But how do we define this winning. President Trump had an answer, "From now on, victory will have a clear definition. Attacking our enemies, obliterating ISIS, crushing Al Qaeda, preventing the Taliban from taking over Afghanistan and stopping mass terror attacks against America before they emerge."

But are these reasonable goals? We can surely obliterate ISIS. But what will stop Islamist extremists from forming a new group bent on destroying Western Civilization? ISIS itself was formed from the scattered remnants of Al Qaeda in Iraq after that group was obliterated.

How are we going to crush Al Qaeda when these terrorist groups metastasize creating Al Qaeda in the Arabian Peninsula (AQAP), Al Qaeda in the Islamic Maghreb and others?

And most directly to the point of President Trump's speech, how are going to prevent the Taliban from taking over Afghanistan. We can, of course, prevent the Taliban from taking over Afghanistan by maintaining a constant military presence to smack down the Taliban whenever it raises its ugly head. But we have been playing Taliban whack-a-mole for 16 long years and still they control almost 40% of the country.

The root of this particular problem is that most of the Taliban are Pashtun. One could actually say the Pashtun are the Taliban because a Pashtun tribesman is more loyal to his fellow tribesman over any government in Kabul so virtually every Pashtun in Afghanistan is a Taliban fighter or a Taliban supporter (because the fighters are fellow tribesmen).

This is why Pakistan is so important in resolving the problems in Afghanistan, because, while there are 11 million Pashtun in Afghanistan (about a third of the population), there are 30 million Pashtun in Pakistan. The border between Afghanistan and Pakistan was created by a British civil servant named Mortimer Durand who created the "Durand Line" separating the two countries. He cared little about the ethnic makeup of the two countries and cared more about creating a buffer area between the British Raj on the Indian subcontinent and Imperial Russia. The Pashtun tribesmen at that time probably didn't care about what some foreign infidel said was the border. As the former president of Afghanistan (and a Pashtun) Hamid Karzai said, it is "a line of hatred that raised a wall between two brothers". The current US-supported government of Afghanistan does not recognize this border.

I know that countries do not like to change their boundaries especially when they have to give up territory but wouldn't it be worth it to try and create an independent Pashtunistan? The colonial powers created a welter of borders and administrations that were just lines on maps in the home office. They thought little or nothing about the indigenes or their cultures and familial ties. The Durand Line was about Russia and Britain, not about the Afghans or the Pashtuns. In fact, if you look up "Afghan "on Wikipedia, you will find that there is actually no such thing as an Afghan. You just have Pashtuns, Tajiks, Uzbeks and many other tribes.

It is the same all across the Middle East (which is really only the Middle East if you are a Westerner). The Kurds are spread out over three countries (Turkey, Iran and Iraq), the Palestinians don't even have a country, just a series of refugee camps. And all these various tribes and peoples supply Islamic fighters to try and kick out Western forces that are there to maintain peace within these imaginary boundaries thought up by the French and the British.

It would be wistful thinking that there could be a conference among all these feuding nations and tribes to try and redraw the borders of what we Westerners now call the Middle East. There are natural resources to divide, territory to carve out, cultural and religious treasures to apportion. And don't forget that Shia and Sunni Muslims don't get along very well. Add it all up and you have one unholy mess. Of course, even if it were possible to negotiate new reasonable boundaries the area might still be an unholy mess. But what we are doing now isn't working.

Lacking a regional consensus conflict is likely to continue in the Middle East and South Asia for the foreseeable future. The best that we can hope is the creation of strong governments that have the will and ability to control the violence. These regimes are unlikely to be democracies as we define it. More likely they will be military rulers or hereditary monarchs backed up by tribal councils. Democracy doesn't work when the peoples' loyalties are to tribe and religions over country. When your loyalty is to your Pashtun speaking Pakistani fellow tribesman and not to your Tajik fellow citizen you do not have the solidarity needed to forge a nation except through force (that was Saddam's strategy).

I know developing a regional consensus would be extremely difficult. It may even be impossible to create

Pashtunistan. And it is something that has to be done by the people of this region. Our Western Enlightenment sensibilities won't work there. And the end result may not be something that we particularly like. But that's not the point. We might have the power but we don't have the right to impose a solution on these people (as the British attempted to do but failed). But a unified Pastunistan (even one controlled by the Taliban) would be much easier to deal with than the agglomeration of tribes that make up current Pakistan and Afghanistan. That would not be a win. But it might be a win/win. In the meantime we fight.

2018 Perspective. Amy Chua, in her recent book, *Tribal Politics* (2018) asserts that tribalism and democracy don't mix. Trying to overlay democracy on tribal culture will only lead to injustice, conflict and potentially genocide. This is why we must fight the rising tide of tribalism (which we call identity politics) in America.

September 2017

BernieCare is Your Right

September 15, 2017
Victor C. Bolles

Photo: Nick Solari

The egregiously inept attempt by Republicans to repeal and replace Obamacare has led us to this. Earlier this week, Independent Senator Bernard Sanders (I-Vermont), who describes himself as a democratic (note lower case d) socialist, introduced a bill to convert American healthcare to a single-payer system. He tried to do this before in 2013 but his proposed bill made nary a ripple in Congress back then. So what's different this time?

The difference this time is that 16 Democratic Senate (upper case D) colleagues have signed on as co-sponsors of the proposed bill (compared to 0 previously). Among these co-signers are several potential presidential candidates for the 2020 presidential election (Elizabeth Warren, Corey Booker and Kamala Harris, among others). The Dems think they have found an issue that will help them wrest control of the Congress and the White House from the Republicans. It was Republican ineptitude that handed this issue to them on a silver platter.

They are going to cloak this issue in the American flag and try to convince us that universal healthcare is a basic human right and as American as apple pie and baseball. But wait a minute. What about food and shelter? If healthcare is a basic human right, shouldn't food and shelter also be human basic human rights? Food and shelter are even more basic than healthcare. Shouldn't the Democrats also push for government provided food and shelter? Oh, they will. But that is for future campaigns.

Senator Sanders and his progressive pals will insist that all the other major countries have single-payers systems so why should we keep an American system that is so archaic and dysfunctional? But America is the leader of the free world and leading means doing things differently than the followers. And as for dysfunctionality we must rely on the words of Winston Churchill who said that the Americans can be counted on to do the right thing after they have tried everything else. The reason that the Republicans failed so miserably was that they lacked boldness in their efforts to reform healthcare, settling instead to trying to rejigger an entitlement without calling it an entitlement. Maybe the next time they will do the right thing (finally).

But how does this right to healthcare arise? The right to healthcare is a so-called positive right (also called an entitlement). What I am more familiar with as our rights are now called negative rights (also called liberties). For the rest of our discussion we will use the descriptors positive and negative when referring to rights in order avoid confusion.

A negative right (or liberty) bars others from interfering with you or blocking you from taking some action. The Bill of Rights is full of negative rights (I guess they thought that calling it the Bill of Negative Rights wouldn't sound as good thus leading to our current confusion). (The same would also apply to Life, Negative Right and the pursuit of Happiness.) The government cannot ban our speaking out or oppose our practicing a religion. If our country was conceived in liberty as Abraham Lincoln said then it was conceived in negative rights.

We are also endowed with certain positive rights. If someone tries to block our ability to speak out we have the right to demand that the government prevent that person from blocking our assertion of our negative right. Positive rights can also arise by contract. If I buy a car with a warranty I have a positive right (in other words I am entitled) to have any defect repaired.

The Founders conceived of our "rights" as derived from natural rights because they are universal and inalienable (they cannot be taken away). Enlightenment philosopher John Locke envisioned that people had natural rights even when existing in a pre-societal state of nature. When people enter into a social contract with other human beings to form a society they contractually agree that their natural rights are limited by the natural rights of others. Our American Social Contract entitles us to the positive right that others have the duty to respect our (negative) rights. Many philosophers believe that human rights are natural rights (and therefore are negative rights).

Some people believe that human rights include positive rights. The first 21 articles of the United Nations' Universal Declaration of Human Rights are natural and negative rights. The remaining 9 articles are considered cultural and economic rights some of which could be construed as positive rights. The problem with positive rights is that they entail an obligation on others to take action in order to achieve the positive right.

Senator Sanders and the Democrats assert that people have a positive right to healthcare services because it is a human right. But the means to achieve this positive right requires others (you and me as taxpayers) to provide the financial resources necessary to achieve the goal of universal healthcare (a point which Senator Sanders failed to discuss when he unveiled his proposed bill). We can see that this interferes with our natural right to our own property (the income we have earned or the accumulated wealth we have saved). Locke conceived of property as one of the most important rights because if you do not have right to keep what you have created you really have no rights at all.

So the demand for universal healthcare is not a human right, it is a usurpation of the negative rights of one group (to dispose of their property as they see fit) for the benefit of another group. This is not one of the principles on which our country was founded. In fact, the Founders purposefully included checks on the tyranny of the majority (the ability of the majority to dictate terms unfavorable to a minority).

This is the thing that separates America from the other large economies and their single-payer healthcare systems. Unlike other countries, the United States was founded based on certain principles based on our natural rights. If we discard those principles in order to provide healthcare or any other entitlement (I mean positive right), are we still America? Further, does the extension of "human rights" stop at healthcare or go on to include all the other aspects of our economy (that's called socialism but, heck, Bernie is an avowed socialist).

Before we take such a drastic step (and it is a very drastic step off a precipice) are we not obligated to try and fix healthcare (and other dysfunctional sectors of our society) by faithfully applying the principles on which we were founded? This is a difficult challenge but one that faithfully preserves the <u>idea</u> (emphasis added) of America.

2018 Perspective. The Democratic Socialist Party (including Democratic primary winner Anastasia Ocasio-Cortez who is a member) asserts the right to healthcare in its platform and recommends a single payer system to assure that (positive) right.

Reaganesque? Not Quite.

September 21, 2017
Victor C. Bolles

On Tuesday, September 19, 2017 US President Donald Trump gave his first speech to the General Assembly of the United Nations. President Trump's supporters were effusive in their praise while his opponents denounced it as "bombastic", an "abdication of values". Hillary Clinton described it as "very dark" and "dangerous". Venezuela's clueless foreign minister thought he was insulting Trump by comparing him to Ronald Reagan (he wasn't).

In his speech, President Trump defined "America First" as "renewing this founding principle of sovereignty. Our government's first duty is to its people, to our citizens -- to serve their needs, to ensure their safety, to preserve their rights, and to defend their values." He went on to say, "I will always put America first, just like you, as the leaders of your countries will always, and should always, put your countries first."

President Trump went on to say, "All responsible leaders have an obligation to serve their own citizens, and the nation-state remains the best vehicle for elevating the human condition. But making a better life for our people also requires us to work together in close harmony and unity to create a more safe and peaceful future for all people."

The Wall Street Journal thought that President Trump's foreign policy based on sovereignty was too narrowly construed. The president had said, "We do not expect diverse countries to share the same cultures, traditions, or even systems of government but we do expect all nations to uphold these two core sovereign duties, to respect the interests of their own people and rights of every other sovereign nation." The Editorial Board of the Wall Street Journal felt that other countries should respect the rights of their citizens. But many countries have a different view of what the rights of their citizens are. Over fifty Islamic and majority Muslim countries have signed the Cairo Declaration on Human Rights in Islam rather than the UN's Universal Declaration of Human rights (which apparently aren't so universal). The Soviet Union (now Russia) refused to sign. China signed, but it was the Republic of China (Taiwan) that signed – not the Peoples Republic of China.

When I heard President Trump describing sovereign nations acting in their own interests and in the interests of their citizens, I thought of Adam Smith and how human beings interacted with each other. In the Wealth of Nations he wrote, "It is not from the benevolence of the butcher, the brewer, or the baker that we expect our dinner, but from their regard to their own interest." That is the beauty of the free market economic system as described by Smith. As long as the butcher, the brewer and the baker operate within the rule of law we do not care what their motives are or even if they are nice people and treat their mothers well.

That sounds similar to the foreign policy announced by President Trump where we don't care if other nations have different forms of government (as in dictatorships) or whether they trample the human rights of their citizens (presumably for their own good). But the analogy only goes so far. In Smith's village (Kirkcaldy) the butcher, the brewer and the baker operate within the rule of law because they are required to do so. If they adulterate their products people will shun their offerings. If they cheat their customers they can be arrested by the constable. If their products harm their customers they can be sued in court for damages. Their motives are irrelevant but their actions are not. There are consequences for their bad actions.

The problem with the Trump foreign policy based on national sovereignty and interests is that there are no consequences for bad actions unless they directly affect a country's citizens. Each country defends its rights and its citizens and everyone else has to look out for themselves. Our enlightened world ruled by law as envisioned by John Locke is in danger of becoming a Hobbesian state of nature where life is "nasty, brutish and short."

For seventy years since the end of the Second World War, the United States has been the enforcer of the world's rule of law. Without an enforcer the rule of law breaks down.

I have lived in countries where the rule of law is weak and have seen first hand the impunity of corrupt officials, the oppression of crooked police and the sullenness of the dispirited people.

Who will be the enforcer of the global rule of law under President Trump's America First policy? Don't say the United Nations. The United Nations has no armed forces. When it intervenes it uses the armed forces of its member nations. This can be helpful in minor skirmishes such as during the civil war in Liberia but have been of limited value in the Congo and South Sudan. And the UN cannot be an enforcer of a global rule of law when two non-signatories of the Universal Declaration of Human Rights have the power to veto any action the UN takes.

Since the United Nations accepts all nations and all cultures as members, the UN is essentially valueless. Some of the worst human rights violators are members of the UN's Human Rights Council including Russia, China, Venezuela and Cuba. The UN not only has little ability to enforce a global rule of law, as an institution it has no true concept of what that law should be.

For better or worse, the United States has been the enforcer of the global rule of law for seventy years. Of course, it is an American vision of the rule of law made up of a network of global institutions that reinforce this vision and that is backed up by American military power. Some regimes think this is insufferable meddling much like how street gangs think of beat cops. But the citizens of the neighborhood respect and applaud the cops for their protective presence.

The cost of acting as the world's cop and the enforcer of the rule of law is high both in terms of the lives of our troops and the wealth that we must spend. And President Trump is right that friends and allies should do more to help bear this burden but when push comes to shove if other nations fall short in supporting the rule of law then we must step forward. This is not a situation where, if we are unhappy, we can take our ball and go home. It is true that the cost of acting as the enforcer of the rule of law is high but the cost of having no enforcer would be unbearable.

In his speech President Trump also said, "If the righteous many do not confront the wicked few, then evil will triumph. When decent people and nations become bystanders to history, the forces of destruction only gather power and strength." He went on to lambaste North Korea (a direct threat to the US), Iran (an indirect threat) and Venezuela (not a threat). But the question is: what if it boils down to the righteous few? There are many in the UN that oppose us and more that wouldn't do anything to help us.

But President Trump's words were confusing and contradictory. Are we looking out only for ourselves or are we going to root out the wicked (whether they be few or many)? Deception and confusion may be good tactics in a poker game or when negotiating a business deal but not so much when you are leader of the free world. People need to know that your words mean something and that your actions back up your words. Even President Trump's White House staff can't explain what he is doing and thinking. How are the American people going to understand? How are foreign leaders who have never read The Art of the Deal (and some with their fingers on nuclear triggers) going to react?

Our friends and allies need and deserve more than just the occasional military strike or economic sanction, they need to know that they (and the rest of the world) have the commitment of the United States to honor and enforce, if necessary, the global rule of law. It is this commitment that assures our friends and warns our enemies. Without such a commitment, President Trump is tempting the malevolent actors on the world stage to test America's resolve. It is an invitation to chaos and destruction.

2018 Perspective. President Trump continues to restructure the world order with a wrecking ball. Allies and enemies (as well as the American people) are dazed and confused. How this new world order will look or function we don't know yet. But it will be "great."

This is Dumb!

September 25, 2017
Victor C. Bolles

photo: Ray Terrill

It was bad enough when divisive politics afflicted movie stars and television personalities but then we are accustomed to Hollywood glitterati jetsetting off to a conference on the environment or climate change, spewing tons of carbon from their private jets while lecturing us on how we have to change our lifestyles to save the planet. But now it is getting serious. Now we can't even watch a NFL football game without having to make a decision about whether the team or the player is sufficiently politically correct or incorrect.

2017: A Trumpian Year in Review

President Trump is telling his supporters to boycott the NFL until the owners start firing protesting players. So I guess that means that left-wing Democrats and progressives will be scooping up discounted season tickets to show their support for the protestors. Of course, this means that the tailgate parties will have to change. Out with beer and BBQ, in with watercress sandwiches and chardonnay.

Do you know what you are really doing? Everyone is making this fuss about what Donald Trump said or did. And that is exactly what he wants (I was going to make a comment about Br'er Rabbit but most of you wouldn't know what I was talking about). He is the center of attention. Everybody is focused on him instead of the game. This is exactly what he did during the presidential campaign. He would do something outrageous and that was all that anybody could talk about. He didn't dominate the news - he was the news.

Most of the outraged people don't even know who Colin Kaepernick is or why he sat down during the national anthem. The original issue is irrelevant because now the issue is Trump. All the rage and fury on both side just feeds his enormous ego. I don't think he even cares if you like him or not, as long as your every waking thought is about him.

You could say that I am part of this foolish herd because I am writing another essay about President Trump. But I'm not. I am writing this about you. You are the one letting this person dominate your life and thoughts. Ruining friendships and breaking apart families. This isn't even about politics. Left/right – who cares? This is all about Trump.

The American flag and the national anthem are supposed to be symbols of unity but they are now mere tools used for the feeding of President Trump's ego. He doesn't care if you rage against him. He doesn't care if you are a supporter or opponent. He doesn't care if you hate him or adore him. Every time you post an outrageous comment or dumb joke you are just giving him more of what he wants.

So after I post this essay I am not going to think about Donald Trump for the rest of the day. Anytime a Trump thought tries to edge into my consciousness I will say out my mantra and clear my head. Every time somebody posts about him I will say my mantra again. Repeating and repeating until I can think of something else – anything else. And tonight I am going to watch the Cowboys play football and I don't care who stands, sits or kneels. And if the announcers start to talk about it I will hit the mute button and watch the game in silence.

2018 Perspective. I tried to discover how many times President Trump is the topic of a news article or TV show but I was unable to do so. Most of the hits from my search engine (guess which one) were the ratio of negative to positive coverage and how that ratio differed from that of President Obama. I don't want to know the slant of the coverage (because I already know that – it is very apparent). I don't think President Trump cares about the slant of the coverage either. Because it is still coverage. That's what he really wants.

October 2017

The Nudger Laureate

October 9, 2017
Victor C. Bolles

Dr. Richard Thaler has been awarded the Nobel Prize in Economics (actually the Swedish National Bank's Nobel Memorial Prize in Economic Science since the prize was not included in Alfred Nobel's will) for his work in behavioral economics. He is best known to the general public for his book, Nudge, which he co-wrote with Cass Sunstein, a Harvard professor who worked in the Obama White House (and is married to Obama UN Ambassador, Samantha Power).

Sunstein said of Thaler, "I don't think there's an economist alive who's had as large an impact on the economics profession and the world as Thaler. His influence on public policy and law is so great that people who have never heard the name Thaler and wouldn't be able to say what behavioral economics is are marching to the beat of his drum."

Here is what I said about Professors Thaler and Sunstein in my book, *Principled Policy*.

2017: A Trumpian Year in Review

Many of the scientific advances discussed in this book about how we think and act, both politically and economically, are fairly recent. We have discovered that we don't always act rationally and that we can sometimes be easily manipulated. The work of Professor Kahneman and other economic behaviorists has given us greater insight into ourselves; however, more work needs to be done.

Politics and economics are closely linked. Philosophers of the 17th and 18th century such as Adam Smith studied the political economy. More modern economic theories have tried to separate politics and economics;

however, recent studies have shown that they are inextricably linked.

The thought processes we use to make economic decisions are very similar to those we use for political decision-making. Greater understanding into the psychology of decision-making is essential to the process of improving the functioning of our democracy. Like all knowledge, this understanding can be used for good or evil. We know that advertisers use many tricks to get us to buy their products. We are aware of the concept but are often unaware when these tricks are being used to manipulate our decision-making. Everyone hates attack ads that proliferate at every election cycle, but they keep on coming. They keep on coming because they work.

The research on human behavior will continue. We just need to make sure that this information is public. We have a better chance to protect ourselves from misuse of this knowledge if it is widely known. The concept of democracy has come into question recently and democracy in many countries is threatened. Dictators like the Castro brothers or Kim Jung Un are relatively easy to identify and isolate. Manipulators of democracy like Putin, Chavez, Maduro and Correa use the forms of democracy to stay in power. They actually win elections by using the powers of the state to manipulate people to vote for them. They control the media. Independent voices are isolated and often imprisoned on phony charges. The Internet is censored.

While these international despots are relatively easy to spot we have manipulators in the United States as well (many of which are not so apparent to us). Richard Thaler and Cass Sunstein wrote a very scary book called Nudge. Nudge has a subtitle of "Improving Decisions about Health, Wealth, and Happiness". They think it is not only acceptable but also laudable to manipulate people into making better decisions. But who defines which decision is better? The manipulators, of course. Thaler and Sunstein think it is not just a good thing but a great thing that could be applied throughout our society.

The thought of a bunch of do-gooders working behind the scene to make me do the "right" things is a truly scary thought. We see these nudgers all around us. The abortion of a fetus is converted into a woman's right to choose to take away the sting of death. Homosexuals are converted into gays to make them appear friendly and approachable. Charity and the dole are converted into entitlements to ease the shame of having to take handouts. All these are done to make things more palatable. Entitlements have even gone through a second conversion. Regular government expenditures (mandated by the Constitution) are discretionary parts of the budget, while entitlements (transfers of wealth) are non-discretionary.

You can agree or disagree with particular policy decisions. But let's describe them accurately so that we can make a reasoned decision. We need to shine a bright light on manipulation wherever we find it. We also must structure our democracy in order to resist manipulation. Manipulation is tinkering with the level playing field and, as noted previously, the level playing field (the equality of opportunity) is essential to the democratic social contract that is the United States.

2017: A Trumpian Year in Review

Left/right it does not matter. Everyone is trying to manipulate you. President Trump's digital director, Brad Parscale, explained on 60 Minutes (Sunday October 8th) how he used social media to direct ads designed to appeal to specific groups of targeted voters (especially in swing states). So unless you want to be unknowingly marching to the beat of Professor Thaler's drum (or somebody else's drum) you need to become more aware of the manipulation that is going on around you.

2018 Perspective. It is very clear by now that the Russians planted ads and messages on social media in order to try and manipulate the 2016 elections. Although Facebook and others have taken steps to block such attempts malefactors will certainly try to influence US politics in the future, especially with the 2018 elections coming up. Everyone needs to double-check the newsfeeds they follow for accuracy and authenticity.

Catatonica

October 31, 2017
Victor C. Bolles

The streets of Barcelona are inundated by crowds numbering in the hundreds of thousands alternately demanding secession from Spain and pleading for unity with Spain. So far the secessionists have tried to use the ballot box to declare their independence from Spain but the flawed referendum was largely boycotted by Catalans that believe they are Spanish first.

But the Catalan dilemma is hardly unique. The Basques have been trying to create an independent country for more than a century, sometimes resorting to violence. But the Scots also recently held a referendum to separate from Great Britain. The bonds that hold Walloon and Flemish speaking peoples of Belgium are fraying. Czechoslovakia broke into the Czech and Slovak republics. And let's not forget Brexit.

Is Europe breaking apart? Is this the culmination of a process of greater independence and freedom or the harbinger of the end of Western Civilization as we know it?

The problem is that the Europeans have nothing to hold them together. They have different cultures and different languages. Only the Nordic countries and Britain have a long democratic tradition. Much of the rest was under the sway of monarchs and princes that had aspirations of empire but no common vision to unite its peoples.

Even the glue of the Christian religion is fading from Europe. Church attendance is feeble and many European churches have more tourists than believers. When my wife and I were in Paris she insisted on going the Notre Dame for mass on Sunday but was horrified to discover that the attendance was only about a hundred people that were dwarfed by the enormous cathedral that engulfed them.

French philosopher Pierre Manent, in his book *Beyond Radical Secularism*, asserts that declining religiosity and increasing secularism is the root cause of Europe's problems. Church attendance is lowest among European nations having the most entrenched social welfare systems such as France, Germany, Denmark, Sweden and Norway.

Declining religiosity combined with cradle to grave social welfare has led to the breakdown of social cohesion of the nation states of Europe. The European Union is an economic concept that creates no bond of affection amongst the inhabitants. Even concepts such as France and Spain are unraveling. People are seeking bonds based on language, ethnicity and local culture because their countries are not based on universal principles about which all citizens can agree.

I suppose this would be okay if we inhabited a peaceful world where people could group together as they please and not have to worry about their neighbor. But unfortunately, the world is not peaceful and the future of Europe is now under the gravest threat to its existence since the end of World War II. NATO is our bulwark against encroaching threats. Would NATO be stronger with the inclusion of Catalonia, Wallonia, Vasconia, Scotland and a slew of other little provinces? There are larger forces at work than the provincial interests of the Catalans, Basques, Scots and others.

There is even talk of secession in the United States. A group called CalExit is trying to get a referendum on the secession of California from the United States on the 2018 ballot. But our situation is different than Europe's. While the decline of Christianity and the growing bureaucracy of the European Union have combined to enervate the nation states of Europe, the United States has a common bond from our Founding Principles.

More diverse than any European nation state, the United States has been held together by our Founding Principles over ethnicity or religion. California's desire to leave the Union (or at least the desire of some Californians) is due to ideology. These irate Californians do not agree with the Founding Principles of America. They are more comfortable with the Marxist-based socialism of Bernie

Sanders than the aspirations of Washington, Jefferson and Franklin.

The lust for state-provided welfare benefits in combination with moral equivalency is eroding belief in our American Founding Principles just as they are breaking down the bonds holding our European allies together. In this age of rising global tension, the need for unity is greater than ever. The progressive advocates of doing "what works" to relieve life's burdens, even on people capable of bearing them, has the unintended consequence of sapping the will of the so-called beneficiaries.

The internal problems that afflict us are not caused by our Founding Principles but by our inability to live up to them and our penchant for electing leaders who don't even aspire to live up to them - leaders who pitch principles into the trash bin when they interfere with the ability to raise campaign funds or to buy votes with welfare benefits.

We need a national renewal and recommitment to our Founding Principles. We need a recommitment to the equality of opportunity to provide hope for a better future. We need a recommitment to the equality of justice for all. We need a recommitment to the free market economics that has provided us with nature's bounty and technological wonders. We need this rededication to the American Spirit or we will end up like Catatonica. Or worse.

2018 Perspective. The purveyors of identity politics on both the left and the right denigrate our Founding Principles in order to promote identity based on ethnic, gender, language or other identity. Little do they realize what they are destroying in order to push their agendas. An independent Catalonia would be unlikely to send its armed forces to the defense of Spain, let alone an amorphous entity such as Europe. Separately we are weak. We are only strong when we are united. Our Founding Principles kept us united and strong though many trials. We cannot afford to discard them now.

November 2017

Making Diversity Work

November 2, 2017
Victor C. Bolles

On October 31st 2017, an immigrant from Uzbekistan, Sayfullo Saipov, mowed down walkers and bicyclists along the West Side Highway bike path, killing eight. Mr. Saipov had entered the United States seven years earlier on a diversity visa.

The Diversity Visa Lottery Program was a part of a bill introduced by Chuck Schumer in 1990 when he was still in the House of Representatives. The diversity lottery was part of a larger immigration bill that was eventually approved with bi-partisan support and signed into law by then President George H.W. Bush. The diversity visa program allows up to 50,000 people per year to obtain an entry visa to the United States and a green card with only minimal qualifications. That's over a million largely un-vetted people over the life of the program. The Diversity Visa Lottery Program is slated to be eliminated by the Trump Administration under the proposed Reforming American Immigration for a Strong Economy Act.

Many of the people that are opposed to the Diversity Visa Lottery Program will be labeled racists and even Islamaphobes. And in many cases that might be correct. But that doesn't make the Diversity Visa Lottery Program a good idea or worthy of being a part of a rational immigration policy.

Many proponents of diversity do not understand how to make diversity work for a society. They want universities and the workplace to "look like America" so they come up with programs, such as affirmative action, to increase the number of minorities in these institutions (the NBA being an exempt institution). At the same time they propose to open the US borders to indiscriminate immigration to change how America looks (probably requiring an expansion of the coverage of affirmative action).

Democrats see diversity as a goal, not as a tool. Take this quote from the Democratic National Committee website:

"Above all, Democrats are the party of inclusion. We know that diversity is not our problem--it is our promise. As Democrats, we respect differences of perspective and belief, and pledge to work together to move this country forward, even when we disagree. With this platform, we do not merely seek common ground--we strive to reach higher ground."

The definition of what this higher ground consists of is left undefined. If diversity is a promise what is it promising? Apparently just more diversity and a Democrat in the White House and majorities in the House and Senate (60+).

People come to America for two principal reasons: economic opportunity and freedom from oppression. The economic opportunity in America is derived from our free market economic system that has been so successful over the last two hundred years. And economic freedom and opportunity are intimately entwined in our personal liberty enshrined in our Constitution and Founding Principles. Can diversity help us achieve these goals?

It can! If done correctly. University of Michigan political science and economics professor, Scott E. Page described mathematically in his book, *The Difference*, how diversity can help to achieve optimal results in problem solving. But it is purposeful diversity to achieve a common goal. He also noted that it is thought diversity that can achieve these results, two different ways to looking at a problem. Thus an economist and a mathematician would have a better probability of solving a problem than two economists or two mathematicians. He also noted that an economist and a beautician might not achieve a better result if the beautician didn't have the proper skill sets to solve the problem.

Ray Dalio, the billionaire CEO of Bridgewater Capital, described a similar process in his book, *Principles*. He recommends a business practice that employs radical truth and radical transparency to achieve a diversity of thought that is subjected to believability weighting in order to achieve an idea meritocracy that delivers superior results.

Both processes rely on two fundamental principles to achieve superior results. First and foremost, the goal is agreed upon and the only differences are in how to achieve the desired result. Second, it is diversity of thought (different approaches to solving a common problem) that can achieve the desired goal. Of course, people of different cultures, races and genders will have different ways to solving problems so some diversity along these lines would be helpful.

But this is not diversity for diversity's sake (or for the sake of diverse people). It is diversity to serve a purpose. The purpose of diversity in America should be directed toward achieving the goals of America's Founding Principles, not changing our principles. Diversity working to solve a common problem or achieve a common goal can be very effective. But a diversity of goals is chaos.

We are still reeling from the tragic nature of Mr. Saipov's crime and I hesitated in using him as an example. But the Diversity Visa Lottery Program has now become a political issue so I thought it was important to insert a reasoned and rational discussion of this program and why it makes little sense and should be eliminated.

2018 Perspective. In the run up to the 2018 election, Democrats are pushing the idea of eliminating ICE (Immigration and Customs Enforcement). They apparently want to allow open borders so that whoever wants to emigrate to America can do so without restriction. But a country without a border is no country. It's just a plot of land.

The Elephant in the Room

November 17, 2017
Victor C. Bolles

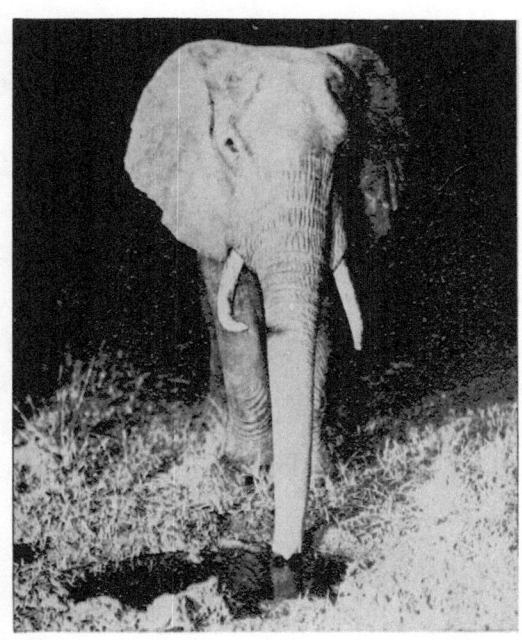

There has been much hyperbolic discussion on both the left and the right about the proposed GOP tax reform and tax cut. Most of the discussion is about who wins and who loses. The Democrats assert that the one-percenters are reaping fistfuls of underserved money off the backs of the poor. The Republicans counter that the tax cuts are aimed at the middle-class and the simplified tax code requires only a postcard size (the millennials ask "what's a postcard?") tax return. The media outlets loudly repeat the same according to their proclivities by parading a plethora of partisan talking heads in front of the public.

Everyone is talking like the government is some sort of gift shop where everyone goes to get presents and goodies. But all this discussion ignores the most important thing. Taxes are the public's obligation to fund the government so it can operate. To the extent that we are all citizens of this great country, we should all bear an equitable share of this burden.

Taxes, or rather the avoidance of taxes, create powerful incentives and politicians have learned to use the tax code to motivate people to do all sorts of things such as purchase electric automobiles or put money in 401(k)s (although what they principally want to motivate people to do is to vote for the provider of said benefit). Many people consider these benefits good things and most of them are well intended. But all these incentives and benefits stuffed into the tax code ignore the people's obligation to fund the government.

The proposed GOP tax reform goes a long way to reduce the gobbledygook of incentive programs but still retains some of the most egregious abusers such as the mortgage interest deduction (although with some limits). But the fervor of Republicans to reduce taxes is almost equal to the eagerness of Democrats to increase government expenses. Republicans say that we need tax cuts to spur economic growth.

Why the ardent desire to goose the economy? GDP growth is around 3% and the official unemployment rate is down to 4.1%, considered by many to be full employment (although workforce participation is low by historical standards and there are many part-time employees that would prefer a fulltime job). The economy could be a bit better but it is chugging along right now and has been slowly improving. Many economists believe that this slow improvement is the best that the economy can do (the so-called "new normal" as dubbed by Larry Summers) because of changing demographics as baby boomers begin to retire and to the unintended consequences of expanded welfare benefits.

The other great howl about the tax reform package (in addition who is laughing all the way to the bank and who is getting screwed) is how much will it cost. The right-leaning Tax Foundation states that the proposed bill would add $516 billion dollars to the deficit over ten years while other estimates put the bill at one to two trillion dollars. But keep in mind that the optimistic cost of around a half a trillion dollars is over and above the nine and a half trillion dollar accumulated deficit over the next ten years as estimated by the Congressional Budget Office.

This is the elephant in the room. A big ten trillion dollar elephant sized increase in our already enormous twenty trillion dollar public debt. This is the thing about costly tax cuts and costly welfare programs. Ultimately, you have to pay for them. In our case we are passing that payment down to our children and grandchildren. The largesse we enjoy for not paying for our current expenses will be a burden on future generations. We are stealing our children's future instead of providing them a better future as our parents and grandparents did for us.

2017: A Trumpian Year in Review

Truth be told we either need to reform Medicare/Obamacare and Social Security or we need to pay for these programs out of current income as well as pay down existing debt. With an expected budget deficit of $487 billion for 2018, that's about $1,500 for every man, woman and child in America. So your typical four-person household owes $6,000 to eliminate the deficit. Pay up. And if we want to reduce the national by half over the next twenty years, that's another $1,500 per person (or $6,000 per family of four). That's not just for 2018. That's every year for the next twenty years. Our grandparents got through the Depression through thrift and we repay that sacrifice with wanton spending.

The one thing that is not mentioned in all this jabber about taxes is whether the country is better for it. The United States will be facing mounting challenges in the coming years and must be militarily strong, financially sound and firm in our commitment to America's Founding Principles in order to be able to meet these challenges. It's time to step up. Call your congressman or woman.

2018 Perspective. Nothing has changed. A booming economy and a rising stock market are reflective of the fact that everyone is blind to our perilous future. Forget calling. Vote for someone who will not ignore this issue. If you can find one.

Progressivism Confronts Human Nature

November 30, 2017
Victor C. Bolles

Photo by: David Shankbone

On Wednesday morning, November 29, 2017 NBC News announced the immediate termination of long-time

Today host Matt Lauer for "inappropriate sexual behavior". What type of inappropriate sexual behavior Lauer committed in not yet known but I would not be surprised to learn that a book deal was in the works.

When right wing icons such as Bill O'Reilly and Roger Ailes are branded as sexual predators the left-wing press (also known as the Mainstream Media) are quick to condemn them with little or no proof. Progressives were aghast when Judge Roy Moore won the Republican primary to replace Jeff Sessions in the Senate but were tickled pink (their favorite color) when they learned of his alleged penchant for young girls (even though a recent visit with relations in the South revealed that a certain person's grandmother got married at the age of 13).

But when the sexual predators turn out to be progressive icons like Harvey Weinstein or a card-carrying member of the media elite like Lauer progressives are confused and distraught. In their simplified world they are the good guys. But good guys are as human as anybody else. I mean OMG. As I write this piece, the World Wide Web newsfeed is telling me that Minnesota Public Radio has fired Garrison Keillor over "allegations of inappropriate behavior" (again undefined). I mean you can't get much more nice guy than Garrison Keillor (a life-long Democrat and Hillary supporter).

The Founding Fathers understood the nature of man and realized that the Hobbesian all-powerful monarch personified by George III can do much evil when seduced by virtually unlimited power. They further realized that the new democratic nation they were creating would give certain men great power and that this power could be easily abused. So they drafted a constitution that included checks and balances against the accumulation of power by a single person or small group of people. These checks and balances make democracy a very messy business. Power is diffuse and even holding both houses of Congress and the Presidency can't guarantee success.

Progressives chafe at this limitation of the power of the state. President Obama used the power of his pen to circumvent the checks and balances created by the Founders. Millennials wanted to elect Bernie Sanders so that he could concentrate even more power in the hands of the state. What can go wrong? Bernie's a nice guy. But what happens when Bernie passes the socialist baton to a successor who is more akin to Stalin or Mao than Mr. Rogers. Millions were sacrificed to their communist concept of how to construct a better world.

The weakness of the progressive agenda is that its implementation is dependent on good intentions. And many people have good intentions – most of the time (despite the fact that some of these well intentioned people are conservative Christians). But even in a socialist paradise there exist people driven by greed and a lust for power. Matt Lauer and Harvey Weinstein were able to prey on women for decades because of the perceived power of their positions. Because all of this sexual harassment and abuse is about power. Power provides immunity. People use harassment and intimidation to enhance and extend their power. It isn't limited to sexual harassment of women although sexual predation is especially effective on women and gives men an additional ego boost. But abuse of power is endemic in all sorts of companies, institutions, organizations and, yes, government. The reason that so many women are coming forth and outing their abusers is not because there is more abuse but there has been a change in the power relationships. Women have discovered that they can fight and defeat their abusers and that's a good thing.

Maybe these recent tawdry affairs will teach our progressive friends some humility. We humans are chained to our human condition, which means that we don't always act reasonably. Sociologists and behavioral economists have shown that there is a strong instinctual element to our human nature that can override our frontal lobes and our best intentions. Giving more power to government will draw abusers and harassers to its flame. Making people dependent on government is only another form of abuse. It is the checks and balances incorporated into our Constitution that have allowed our republic to flourish for two hundred years. They keep the abusers at bay and provide a pathway to reform and renewal.

Many people are worried about our republic because despite our checks and balances the abusers have found cracks in our protections to worm their way into the very fabric of our country. We are in desperate need of reform and renewal. But the answer does not lie in concentrating more power in the hands of the state.

2018 Perspective. New revelations are published on a practically daily basis. 160 women testified about the abuse they endured from Team USA Gymnastics doctor Larry Nasser. 160! How could this abuser continue abusing women for decades? Some men try to downplay these accusations. Some accusations are probably false. But the enormity of the revelations against seemingly well-respected men (and some women) reveals something important about humanity (because I don't think this is limited to the United States). I believe a change in how people think about these situations and what needs to be done about it is going to occur and it will be important.

December 2017

Wagner's Sad Law

December 5, 2017
Victor C. Bolles

While sipping my morning coffee early Monday, I watched an interview of former Clinton Treasury Secretary and Harvard President Emeritus Larry Summers on CNBC's Squawk Box. He expounded on an op-ed piece he had written for the Washington Post that claimed that thousands would die each year because of the GOP's tax bill that had passed the Senate over the weekend. It seemed very sad that Mr. Summers might be correct in his assumption. But my reason for being so sad was for a very different reason than that which provoked Mr. Summers' op-ed.

Mr. Summers explained to hosts Becky Quick, Joe Kernan and Ken Langone, "I think this bill is very dangerous. When people lose health insurance, they're less likely to get preventive care, they're more likely to defer health care they need, and ultimately they're more likely to die."

What Mr. Summers omitted to say was that when people lose health insurance that they don't pay for, they're less likely to do all those healthful things necessary to extend their lives. If you gave them, cash and suggested that they use it to purchase health insurance they are more likely to buy a flat panel TV and a case of beer to watch the Super Bowl. So it must be, by Mr. Summers' way of thinking, the government's job to provide health insurance (or force companies to provide it)

Mr. Summers is a believer in big government. New York Times columnist David Leonhardt pointed out that in a September speech in Washington Mr. Summers had updated Wagner's Law by stating that the United States was destined to ever bigger government due to; 1) an aging population of retirees, 2) the need to reduce income inequality, 3) the increased need for labor intensive services in education and healthcare, and 4) increased defense spending because we live in a dangerous world (well he's right about number 4 thanks to President Obama).

Wagner's Law, for you benighted folks who believe in free enterprise, is the theory of an obscure German economist named Adolph Wagner (1835-1917) who stated that public expenditure (as a percent of GDP) grows as national wealth increases (don't feel bad, I had not heard of it either). Wagner was a proponent of state socialism, which would be the result of ever increasing state expenditures (an outcome that I would agree would be inevitable).

But ever increasing state expenditure is more like sickness than an economic truism (and socialism a form of economic death). The fever we get with the flu is a symptom that tells us our body is in need of healing. The ever increasing state expenditure makes the population ever more dependent on government for basic services. This is a sickness in our society and we need to reevaluate causes in order to develop cures.

More than fifty years after President Johnson announced the War on Poverty there are as many poor as in 1964. But poverty is relative. The poor today have much more material wealth than the poor of 1964 (as well as the poor of other countries). But more than relative material poverty, the poor today have a poverty of self-esteem. Prior to the welfare state, poor people had to work to survive. The working poor may have had to struggle to make ends meet but did so with a sense of pride. Many people in our middle-class arose from the working poor. They did so through hard work, the savings of their parents and education to better themselves.

The poor today are fraught with a sense of hopelessness. Progressives will tell us that the poor have a sense of hopelessness because the system is rigged against them. And they are right. The social welfare system in the United States is designed to keep the poor in a state of hopelessness and low self-esteem that makes them ever more dependent on the state for the material necessities of life. But the state cannot give them pride in their own accomplishments or the self-esteem from doing a job well.

Mr. Summers also noted on Squawk Box that while the average longevity of Americans is increasing the longevity of the wealthy is increasing much faster than that of the poor. But a review of the principal causes of why this is occurring does not include poverty or the lack of health care. The New York Times noted that the wealthy have largely given up smoking while the poor continue the habit and that this fact alone may explain as much as a third of the disparity in longevity. Add in drug addiction and homicide rates among the poor and even more of the disparity is explained.

Another unintended consequence of the social welfare system has been the increase in single parent families. A fatherless (or motherless) household must exert enormous effort to not fall into a well of despair. Single parent families are much more likely to be on welfare and receive food stamps. The health consequences for children in single parent families, while not pre-ordained, are dire.

Even the New York Times notes, "Limited access to health care accounts for surprisingly few premature deaths in America, researchers have found. So it is an open question whether President Obama's health care law -- which has sharply reduced the number of Americans without health insurance since 2014 -- will help ease the disparity (thus refuting Mr. Summers' original contention - by the New York Times no less)."

Yet still progressives (Mr. Summers numbered among them) insist that more government involvement is necessary to fix a situation that, if not caused by government interference, at the very least has not been helped by government involvement. So it is very sad that millions of Americans are so depressed in spirit by the government's oppressive and smothering control over their lives that they care little about the consequences of their actions even if it shortens their lives - the same fate that befell the Soviet proletariat. That is sad.

2018 Perspective. The Cato Institute study by John Early (Reassessing the Facts about Inequality, Poverty and Redistribution) noted that welfare payments and other transfers have greatly reduced poverty while not lifting up the poor from their dependency. This is the antithesis of America's Founding Principles that are intended to make people independent.

Grading the GOP Tax Bill

December 22, 2017
Victor C. Bolles

Well we have a tax bill, and it is even more unpopular than Obamacare was right after it was passed on a purely partisan vote (just as the tax bill was). Only time will truly tell us the impact of this legislation.

During the debate leading up to the passage of this bill I laid out eight principles upon which tax policy should be based. I detail the reasons for the principles in my pamphlet, *A Summation of the Principles of Taxation*. Let's see how this new Tax Cuts and Jobs Act of 2017 compares to the principles I outlined.

1. Taxes should be used to pay for the operations of government. (Grade D-)

The Tax Cuts and Jobs Act clearly does not move us any closer to eliminating the deficit or reducing public debt (the name says it all). In fact it is projected to increase the deficit by $150 billion, a 37% increase in the deficit for 2018. It would be hyperbole to say that paying for the operations of the government were not a consideration of our legislators but it was clearly of secondary importance. The primary goal was to pump up the economy (which is actually chugging along quite nicely) in order to create jobs (see below). The second priority of the tax bill continues to be to manipulate the behavior or citizens in order to achieve government approved goals. Of course 60 percent of expenditures go to entitlements, which are not government operations but transfer payments. Constitutionally obligated government operations are being starved in order to fund these payments.

2. Incomprehensible tax rules undermine the people's trust in government so tax policy should be made understandable to citizens (Grade C)

While numerous deductions have been eliminated, many have been retained. In addition, while the goal of the legislators to normalize the taxes on small business to rates more or less equivalent to big corporations, the new rules on "pass through" income are very complex and confusing (and this is before the IRS begins drafting the actual regulations).

3. It is not possible to create a tax system that will deemed to be "fair" (Grade C).

Republicans think the new tax bill is God's gift while the Democrats think it is the worst tax bill ever. The bill got no Democratic votes. But it is impossible to create a "fair" tax code. Everyone's opinion about how fair the tax bill is personal, not rational. Even people who pay no tax now think it is unfair because other people will pay less. But if Republicans give it an A+ and Democrats give it an F, then the average is C.

4. Payment of taxes is an obligation of citizenship so all citizens should pay some tax. (Grade D)

In the 2012 presidential campaign, Mitt Romney noted that 47% of the population pays no income taxes. This new tax bill will increase that percentage. By doubling the standard deduction Republicans claim that 70% of tax filers will be able to use a simple postcard. Well of course! If you are not paying any income tax filing your "taxes" is easy. But this exemption further attenuates the shared burdens of citizenship that bind this nation together.

5. Tax policy should not be used to manipulate people or organizations. Grade B-

The new tax code eliminates many deductions and replaces them with a larger standard deduction. This will help the poor and lower income tax filers who rarely itemize their taxes and disadvantage the wealthy and those that live in high tax states (mostly Democrats). But it still retains the mortgage interest deduction and hedge fund billionaires can continue with the carried interest deduction (although slightly modified). So the Republicans have come partway along the path to a principled tax policy but they still haven't reached the Promised Land.

6. Cutting taxes is not an effective means of generating long-term economic growth. Grade D.

Politicians distort the original intent of Prof. Keynes. He stated in his theory that increased government spending during a recession would increase aggregate demand and spur an economic recovery even though this would cause an increase in public debt. But he would not have recommended goosing an economy chugging along at 3 percent growth and record low unemployment even though the Fed is tightening monetary policy by raising rates. Washington gets a D because they don't understand how the economy works.

Some pundits may say that the economy is booming and the stock market is hitting record highs in anticipation of the Trump tax cuts. But any boost in economic growth is likely to have been driven by reduced regulation where the Trump administration has been very effective in unwinding the regulatory stranglehold of the Obama administration. Pundits get a D too.

7. Corporate taxes should be competitive with the tax systems of our major trade partners. Grade A-.

The GOP tax bill reduces the corporate tax rate from 35% to 21% which, combined with state taxes that our large trading partners do not have, put it in about the middle of the pack. High corporate tax rates combined with a global tax regime distorted the economic relationship with our trading partners to our great disadvantage. This distortion caused US corporations to not repatriate their foreign earnings resulting in a $3 trillion cash hoard overseas. This cash hoard could be invested in new overseas operations or lent to a US affiliate such that US profits were transferred overseas. Ultimately, some US corporations merged with foreign companies in low tax countries such as Ireland and transferred their legal domiciles (and headquarters staff) to the low tax countries. These so-called tax inversions were labeled unpatriotic and even traitorous but the true villain was not the corporations but the US tax code.

The new tax code changes all that. Democrats assert that the repatriated money will be squandered in stock buybacks and huge dividends instead of invested to create new jobs. But our Democratic friends forget how the free market system works. By putting this money into the hands of investors the capital will reallocated to other companies and projects better able to utilize the funds. And the new tax code lowers the overall cost of capital, which will help marginal projects become profitable. In the long run this will mean more domestic investment, increased GDP and more jobs (keeping in mind that the new plant and equipment will be high tech such that the impact on employment will be muted).

But they also put in a few clauses that mess up an otherwise good story such as the immediate write off of investment in capital equipment (not a bad idea buy why for only five years and for one asset class). That and a few others meant they only earned an A-.

8. Economic growth is stunted by uncertainty so tax policy should not change every year. Grade D.

The Republicans passed the new tax bill with only a simple majority and no bi-partisan support. In order to qualify for a simple majority vote the deficit impact of the bill could not exceed $1.5 trillion over ten years, according to Senate rules. To accomplish this the Republicans made the corporate tax cuts permanent and the personal cuts temporary. But the Republicans assure us that when the ten years are up, they will vote to extend them. But all this legerdemain is nonsense. No Congress can bind a future Congress from making new law. Only the Constitution can do that. So the Republicans end up just looking dumb.

When the Democrats regain control of Congress (which they will eventually do) they can vote for a new completely different tax bill that they can pass on a partisan vote. And while the Republicans and Democrats tack back and forth on opposing tax policies our trading partners as well as economic rivals will be steaming right past us.

Conclusion. Grade C-

The new tax bill is neither as bad as Democrats assert nor as good as Republicans proclaim. It has some good ideas and some dopey ones. The biggest problem of this legislation is that it is not based on sound American principles but on political wrangling. The best thing I can say about the bill is that it replaces the old tax code that was Grade F. The only way to build bi-partisan support and a national consensus is to develop a tax policy consistent with America's Founding Principles.

2018 Perspective. Some of the repatriated earnings that had been stashed overseas were put to use in new investments in the US as well as bonuses and raises to employees. A goodly portion has been applied to stock buybacks and dividends but this money in the hands of investors will be reinvested or spent so that it is still positive for the economy. The goosed economy is going so well that companies are complaining of bottlenecks and labor shortages. This strong economy gave the Trump administration the confidence to embark on a trade war with not only China but also with our allies. At least there will be a lot to write about in 2018.

2017: A Trumpian Year in Review

Putting a Tumultuous Year in Perspective

2017 was the first year of the Trump era, an era of unknown duration and unknowable principles. We are still learning what the Trump Era portends but one thing has become crystal clear. It will be an era devoid of the principles that made America great.

President Trump flies by the seat of his pants, says whatever pops into his head and documents it all on Twitter. He won election by appealing to some of the basest instincts of his supporters and continued to follow through on his campaign promises in his first year in office. For most politicians following through on campaign promises would be a laudable novelty, but candidate Trump's promises were not well crafted as policy but were well crafted to appeal to a core group of supporters. This core of supporters allowed him to dominate a plethora of rivals for the GOP nomination and build up an unstoppable lead. He used this core of supporters to carry the American "flyover" states and won the Electoral College even though he trailed the Democratic candidate in the popular vote. In 2017 now-President Trump sought to validate his election by his pronouncements and actions during the year.

The Democratic candidate, Hillary Clinton, sought to gain the Presidency by making everyone feel guilty if they did not support her to become the first woman president. She attempted to employ the Clinton Foundation's influence and her cronies in the Democratic National Committee to guarantee her coronation despite a lackluster campaign of an unlikeable candidate. A shift to the left was insufficient to stop the Republicans from winning the presidency, both houses of Congress, 33 governorships and the vast majority of state legislators.

But that was so 2016. What about 2017? President Trump and the Republican Party along with Ms. Clinton and the Democratic Party continued the 2016 campaign throughout all of 2017, fighting each other tooth and nail on every policy pronouncement, every bill on the floor of congress, every press briefing and every slip of the tongue. Every bill in Congress faces a straight party line vote, which means the bills will be rescinded and new laws passed when the other party gains control. This is what happened to President Obama's initiatives and it is what will happen if a Democrat succeeds President Trump.

As Amy Chua points out in her new book, *Political Tribes* (2018), both President Trump and the Democratic

Party are promoting populist agendas based on identity politics. President Trump panders to white (especially blue-collar) identity politics by promising to restore blue-collar jobs in the rust belt states and by blocking the immigration of non-whites such as Muslims and Hispanics. Democrats are stoking identity politics by splintering all non-whites (as well as even some white women) into increasingly narrow ethnic, racial and gender groups, each with their own identity-specific agenda.

For most of the history of the United States, the white identity was the national identity. Although the United States was "a nation of immigrants" most of those immigrants were from Europe and are now considered "white" although at the time of their arrival in America many such as the Irish, Italians, Poles and Jews were considered to be less pure than northern Europeans and faced discrimination from the current residents (who were previously immigrants). But the white majority is declining and whites are expected to be a minority sometime around the middle of the twenty-first century. This creates anxiety and angst in the white community, making it vulnerable to populist appeals.

Populist appeals to identity are tearing the country apart (Facebook lists 71 gender options for your profile). And because identity lies deep within the instinctual brain, group attachment is emotional and at times irrational. Studies have shown that children broken randomly into groups not only tend to favor their assigned group but also to have a negative perception of the children in the other groups.

Scott E. Page, in his book *The Difference*, has been able to show mathematically that diversity can help reach optimal solutions. But this optimal solution can only be achieved by working toward a single goal or objective. Lacking a common objective no solution is achieved, only division. Left and right are going in opposite directions. The result will not be optimal.

In my books and essays, I have tried to define common goals and objectives that Americans can all rally around. If we have common objectives, our diversity can work to our great advantage. Unfortunately, President Trump and his sycophantic Republicans supporters as well as the progressive wing of the Democratic Party are creating a profusion of goals and objectives that will only result in chaos. And because identity is emotionally attached to our psyches we get angry when identity is attacked and the potential for violence is very high. Fringe groups on both the left and the right have already resorted to violence and this tendency will only become greater unless we can change course.

I have tried to ground my essays in the Enlightenment philosophical thought that motivated the Founders to conceive of American Independence and our constitutional form of government. These Enlightenment values and principles are what make America America.

Essential Reading

Essential Reading from Principled Policy

The Road to Serfdom, Freidrich Hayek

The Wealth of Nations, Adam Smith

Common Sense, Thomas Paine

Second Treatise of Government, John Locke

The Constitution of the United States

The Declaration of Independence

Democracy in America, Alexis de Tocqueville

This Time is Different, Carmen M. Reinhart and Kenneth Rogoff

The Black Swan, Nassim Taleb

Capitalism, Socialism and Democracy, Joseph Schumpeter

The Commanding Heights, Daniel Yergin and Joseph Stanislaw

Thinking Fast and Slow, Daniel Kahneman

The Great Degeneration, Niall Ferguson

Coming Apart: The State of White America 1960-2010, Charles Murray

A Troublesome Inheritance, Nicholas Wade

Misbehaving, The Making of Behavioral Economics, Richard H. Thaler

A Capitalism for the People, Luigi Zingales

Why Nations Fail, Daron Acemoglu and James Robinson

Essential Reading for Edifice of Trust

The Difference, Scott E. Page

The Clash of Civilizations and the Remaking of World Order, Samuel P. Huntington

A Crude Look at the Whole, John H. Miller

The Unheavenly City Revisited, Edward C. Banfield

The Peloponnesian War, Thucydides

Essential Reading for 2017 – A Trumpian Year in Review

The Righteous Mind, Jonathan Haidt

Sapiens, Yuval Noah Harari

Beyond Radical Secularism, Pierre Manent

Civilization, The West and the Rest, Niall Ferguson

2017: A Trumpian Year in Review

Political Tribes, Amy Chua

About the Author

Victor C. Bolles

Victor is the author of the groundbreaking book, *Principled Policy* that analyses the American Social Contract and builds a framework of how to understand the most important public policy issues of our time. He followed up that important work with *Edifice of Trust*, looking at how the important social issues of our time relate to the American Founding Principles. His new work, *2017 – A Trumpian Year in Review*, is a collection of essays documenting the events of 2017 and looking at them from a principled perspective.

Victor has worked in the Office of Technical Assistance of the US Treasury Department for fifteen years specializing in advising foreign governments on the issuance and management of government debt. He worked throughout Central America and the Caribbean and was resident for eight years in Honduras and El Salvador.

Prior to joining Treasury, Victor was an independent investment banker working out of San Antonio, TX. Victor worked at Citibank for many years in New York, Mexico City, Quito, Ecuador and Lagos, Nigeria where he was head of the investment bank and regional treasurer. His first job after graduate school was with Swiss Bank Corporation (now a part of UBS).

Victor has lived overseas for 16 years, speaks Spanish fluently and has traveled extensively. Victor has an MBA in Finance from the University of Michigan. He is married to Diane and has three children and three grandchildren

(This book and its contents are the sole work of Victor Bolles in his capacity as a private citizen and should not be considered to be a statement of policies or opinions of the Department of the Treasury.)

Read Victor's blog at:
www.edificeoftrust.com/principled-policy-blog
www.edificeoftrust.com